Made for Each Other

Raised in a Jewish family and married to an Anglican clergyman, Michele Guinness is a freelance journalist and P.R. consultant. She has worked extensively in radio and television, for two years presenting her own programme on BBC local radio. Most recently she has been a reporter for Granada Television on ITV's This Sunday. *Her other books include* Child of the Covenant, The Guinness Legend, A Little Kosher Seasoning *and* Tapestry of Voices.

Made for Each Other

Reflections on the opposite sex

MICHELE GUINNESS

TRIANGLE

First published 1996
Triangle
SPCK
Holy Trinity Church
Marylebone Road
London NW1 4DU

British Library Cataloguing-in-Publication Data

A catalogue record of this book is available from
the British Library

ISBN 0-281-04859-2

Typeset by Pioneer Associates Perthshire
Printed in Great Britain by
The Cromwell Press Melksham, Wiltshire

*For Peter, my favourite of all men,
who makes me feel it's good to
be a woman.*

Contents

Introduction

I thought I knew all there was to know about men. After all, I've lived with one or other of the species for most of my life. The truth is I knew as little about them as I suspect they knew about me. This compilation became a voyage of discovery into the secret world of the male. It is my hope that men will also find it a voyage into the mystery of femaleness – so that when we reach our destination, we may end up a little nearer than we were at the start.

Is there really such distance between us? My husband says that when I write or speak I don't always appear to think theologically. I think it's more important to go for the guts. He's banging the drum for accuracy, for categorical statements which are right. I'm trying to make sense of the world by integrating my personal experience with everyone else's. At least, that's what I tell myself. In other words two entirely different, often conflicting sets of logic are in operation.

And that can be true in a mixed group as much as in an individual relationship. I'm part of a team of people whose aim is to bring the best of Christian culture to our city. It's a stimulating, safe sort of group, where the men are sensitive, caring, thoughtful, understanding, very much in touch with their feminine side. We explore gender issues, politics, the arts, the meaning of life, and the place of God in all of it. There we were one evening, ensconced in our usual corner of the local pub, solving the mysteries of the universe. I was holding forth, as I do, being a typical Jewish woman and having what linguistics professor Deborah Tannen calls 'a high-involvement speaking style' (in other words, I'm not exactly backwards at coming forwards). Female sexuality was the subject of conversation, as I remember. A pearl of wisdom was about to fall from my lips when Andy arrived back at the table with the drinks and an earth-shattering revelation: 'Manchester United are two–nil up.' The attention of all four males was immediately diverted to a higher plane. Football robbed them of my gem. It was forced back down my throat and I managed not to choke. After all, what am I? A woman, used to applying biblical wisdom about not wasting one's treasures on certain farmyard creatures who only come into their own when fried up for breakfast.

How do men and women come to terms with each other, with centuries of misunderstanding and mis-communication? When is he being selfish or just mannish? And what's the difference? What are woman's besetting sins? There's no doubt we have ways and means of reducing men to manageable proportions. Are we just a mass of unpredictable hormones, or is he simply frightened of what he can't control? Perhaps the time has come to face each other with some of these questions openly and honestly, acknowledging that the world needs us both, and that without one another it would be a much drearier, if less complicated, place.

I am immeasurably indebted to the gentleman who threw me completely at the end of my *Tapestry of Voices* seminar at the Christian Resources Exhibition in Esher two years ago, when he asked me what four things a woman wanted of a man. I didn't sleep for months thinking about it. I drove my friends insane prying into their personal lives, trying to find out. This book is the result. He has a lot to answer for.

In many ways it wrote itself. I never intended having a section on pain for example, until so many contributors expressed it. Several themes emerged not normally discussed by polite Christians – under the lure of anonymity I suspect: the infatuations of middle age, the confusion men feel about their sexuality, the problems of friendship between the sexes.

Some of the pieces will make you sad, some will make you laugh, some will shock, and some may make you angry. None, I hope, will leave you unmoved or unchanged. Here is a catalogue of our putting our foot in it, and coming back for more, because we know, ultimately, it must be worth it.

I do have to say that at the end of my own journey, now that the book is written, I am much more sympathetic to men than I was at the start, if that doesn't sound unbearably patronizing – which is probably a good thing for the men in my orbit. If I am a different person now – beware, you who enter here. As you embark into the unknown, who can tell what the reading of it might do for you?

I believe that God is calling men and women to a new spirit of mutuality in the eighties and nineties. It is not the call of the fifties for women to submit to men, nor the call of the sixties for men to submit to women. And it is not the call of the seventies to submit to no one and look out instead for 'number one'. It is instead the ancient, enduring call of the Loving Creator for us men and women to submit ourselves to one another out of reverence for Christ – that is, turn to the Living God, so that we might turn to one another without fear and become the agents of love we were created to be.

Gordon Dalbey

1

Come Into the Garden, Maud

Two of far nobler shape erect and tall,
Godlike erect, with native Honour clad
In naked Majestic seemd Lords of all,
And worthie seemd, for in their looks Divine
The image of their glorious Maker shon,
Truth, Wisdom, Sanctitude severe and pure,
Severe, but in true filial freedom plac't;
Whence true autoritie in men; though both
Not equal, as their sex not equal seemd;
For contemplation hee and valour formd,
For softness shee and sweet attractive Grace,
Hee for God only, shee for God in him:

John Milton (1608–74)

Well might Milton wax lyrical about the wonders of the mystical union between the innate gallantry of man and the sweet softness of woman. They were more in his mind, than in actual experience. At thirty-five he married a woman half his age who left him shortly after, and was only persuaded to return for a short spell some three years later. That rather tedious insistence on male superiority was hardly the best way to begin a relationship. Poor old Milton became an early advocate of divorce on the grounds of incompatibility.

The ideal at creation was of course total compatibility. 'I will make man a helper fit for him', says God in the book of Genesis. Woman was no second-class citizen. The Hebrew word for helper is *'esher'*, meaning 'complementary'. It was a perfect fit. Adam and Eve took one look at each other and hey presto! The romance was better than any Mills and Boon. But as Milton discovered to his cost, the course of true love between a man and a woman never has run smooth. One bite of the fruit, one cock-a-snoop at the Creator, and, 'It was all his fault', or 'She made me do it'. Farewell to trust, harmony and intimacy. Enter self-consciousness, vulnerability and insecurity. And that wasn't all. No more freedom to frolic in a garden. The gate slammed shut in their faces. Both were now condemned to hard labour – be it creating a viable economy or raising a family. 'The fall', said Mary Stewart van Leeuwen, 'ripped apart the organic unity of homes and communities and turned us into a society of commuting wage earners (mostly men) and domestically isolated homemakers (mostly women).' In other words, man and woman began to revolve in two entirely different worlds, as if stranded on separate desert islands, rowing across to one another from time to time – when the elements were favourable – meeting only when they could find a suitable place to land.

But underneath this incomplete, unsatisfactory state of affairs would remain a deep wistfulness and longing, fed by a distant memory from a long-forgotten past, of a garden where man and woman lived with God as he intended, in absolute complementariness, loving, giving, naked and unashamed.

The Apple

Eve, smiling, pluck'd the apple, then
Laugh'd, sigh'd – and tasted it again:
'Strange such a pleasant, juicy thing
On a forbidden tree should spring!'

But had she seen with clearer eyes,
Or had the serpent been less wise,
She'd scarce have shown such little wit
As to let Adam taste of it!

Lady Margaret Sackville (1881–1963)

But she did – and regretted the consequences ever since. From almost the beginning of time a natural law came into operation, the fruit of human rebellion, that those created to bring each other maximum comfort would inflict upon each other maximum pain.

Few people manage to capture the exquisite hurt and humour of relationships quite like the Scouse-born poet, Stewart Henderson. His poems, as well as popping up on the GCSE syllabus, have been performed on television, radio and at numerous venues. Stewart is a director of the Greenbelt Christian Arts Festival.

Missing

God, being the Pastor
as well as Creator,
thought it not good
for Adam to be alone.

So He sculpted Eve.
With all His heart
He moulded her
and she breathed His breath.
And when she spoke
elephants and orchids listened.

Adam liked her, even loved her,
but then: looked past her
as he has forever.
When she needed comfort
he regarded her unclean
when she yearned with feelings
more brittle than skin,
he turned over and slept.
When they made love
it was quick,
sometimes silent,
a mute wake
an empty satisfaction,
and afterwards
she bathed alone.

Stewart Henderson

Nothing causes our society such intense inner turmoil as male-female relationships. Art, literature, pop songs, express our yearning for the perfect intimacy forfeited so long ago. We cannot live without the otherness of the opposite sex. Yet we are uncomfortable with our nakedness, and remain solitary, locked up in a closed world, rather than taking the risk of exposing our true selves. Yet perhaps, as this piece reveals, written by a minister's wife at a very difficult time in their marriage, it's only when we are at ease with our real selves that we have anything to offer.

With God All Things are Possible

I long to lie beside you
Peacefully – our hearts touching, knowing,
    At one with each other.

But I seem only to touch the surface,
The rest is locked inside.

I long to touch your brow –
To take away the loneliness
To touch your eyes
Reaching the pain they reveal.

But it seems too inaccessible

I want to put my hand inside your heart
And grasp whatever is causing you distress
To tear it from your flesh
And to hide it forever

But that is not the way to deal with it.

There is a way
A way of love and of patience
Of bearing my own pain
Of crying my own tears

Of holding my longings – and growing
To be free to give you
    what you can receive.

With you O God all things are possible,
But I don't always believe this.

It takes a certain maturity to confront each other without the masks. I recently led a seminar on gender issues in our local Church of England comprehensive school. I divided the sixth form of about 150 into groups of boys and girls. Each could write for a group of the opposite sex any question they liked, and expect a reply. Here are some of the results:

GIRLS TO BOYS

Why are boys so insensitive?
To make us look big in front of our friends.

Why do they not tell their partner when something is upsetting them?
We are men and can handle the situation.

Why do you expect people to clean up after you?
Because girls are willing to clean up. If I was alone and the house was a mess, I'd do it.

Why is it alright for boys but not girls to flirt?
Because men are studs and girls are tarts.

Why do you never talk on the phone?
Because we don't gossip. We've got better things to do – like football.

BOYS TO GIRLS

Why do women think we're only after sex?
Because that's the overall impression we get. Men
   don't communicate enough.

Why don't women make their feelings clear?
We do, but you don't listen or understand.

**Why do you always get so paranoid about your
   lad with other girls?**
Because it takes a long time to trust someone,
   especially boys.

Why do girls show feelings in the wrong situations?
What are 'the wrong situations'? At least we show
   our feelings.

**Why don't women understand our feelings for
   them?**
Because you don't tell us. Say what you mean.

**How come, when something's wrong, girls don't
   tell us but slag us off to their friends?**
We can relate to our friends better.

Why do girls take things to heart so much?
Because we're sensitive and caring.

*And who thought we lived in a brave new world where
mutuality and equality were the order of the day? You can rely
on seventeen-year-olds to give the game away. Most of their*

questions were to do with feelings and problems of communication. Which all goes to show, if we didn't know it already, that government legislation on equality can't change the human heart. In fact it only seems to create a greater dilemma for the men. They're 'incredibly lost, threatened by women who are intelligent, capable and equal', said actress Cherie Lunghi in the Radio Times recently. But before we get carried away on a wave of sympathy, let's meditate on a century of men shirking their share of the chores.

The Swiss psychologist Paul Tournier, one of the first Christian voices to raise gender issues, believed that since the time of the Renaissance, Western civilization had been dominated by cold, objective male values, while the 'feminine' qualities of sentiment, emotion and relationship were dismissed as inferior. That, he maintained, was the reason behind the disappearance of small communities, the emphasis on centralization, the growth of multinationals, the concentration of economic power, and the increase in bureaucracy. Quite an indictment. But retrieve the balance, said Tournier, and the potential is there to make the world a better place.

A little bit overstated perhaps, but it reflects our yearning for the intimacy we once knew in Eden. Can we find our way back into the paradise garden, forgive the bitterness of the past, live in harmony and learn to speak the same language again? Only when we're prepared to work, listen, understand and change. Then we may get a taste of what was and is meant to be. Salvation is ours because of the cross of Christ. So is the responsibility of working out its implications in every aspect of our relationships.

We are fired into life by a madness that comes from our incompleteness. We awake to life tense, aching, erotic, full of sex and restlessness.

This dis-ease is, singularly, the most important force within existence. It is the force for love and we are fundamentally shaped by our loves and deformed by their distortions. . . .

The longing was understood religiously: Adam, missing his rib, longing for Eve, man and woman, woman and man, longing for primal wholeness in God and in each other. . . .

In such a view, we pursued each other, embraced each other, and loved and made love to each other against the horizon of the infinite, under a high symbolic hedge. Love, romance, sex and passion were sacred things, surrounded by much chastity and mystique.

Today the hedge is lower . . . we have trivialised this longing, making it mean something much more concrete. The longing is for the good life, for good sex, for good successes, for what everybody else has, for the sweetening of life. . . . We no longer see our longing as a congenital and holy restlessness put in us by God to push us towards the infinite. . . .

And so we should ask ourselves the question: What kind of lovers are we?

Ronald Rolheiser

In Eden, the yearning of the woman for harmony with her man continued after disobedience. Yet the man did not reciprocate: instead, he ruled over her to destroy unity and pervert sexuality. Her desire became his dominion. But in the Song of Songs, male power vanishes. His desire becomes her delight. Another consequence of disobedience is thus redeemed through the recovery of mutuality in the garden of eroticism.

Phyllis Trible

13

When a man and a woman truly love each other, whether it be through the tenderness and communion of marriage or in celibacy and community life, there is nothing more beautiful. It is the gift of God to humanity. Their love is the root of the 'body' which is the community. It is the power of unity which will inspire all other unities; it is the power of healing which will inspire all other healings. It is fruitful with a spiritual fruitfulness.

Jean Vanier

2

Let's Play Mums and Dads

No one ever warns you about the effect of becoming a parent on the relationship between a man and a woman. For the first two weeks after our son was born, my husband ran round the kitchen like a headless chicken opening packets and reading instructions: the sterilizing solution, the nappy disinfectant, the feed, the gripe water, the baby shampoo. I think it's probably a throw-back to the good old days when the men, as soon as their wives were in labour, were sent to boil gallons of water. No one to this day know why, except that it kept them preoccupied and out of mischief. Men, as all women know, need something to do in a crisis. It calms their nerves and makes them feel useful. It's at childbirth that for the first time in the relationship he may feel a spare part, an observer, shut out.

Child-rearing can either enhance a sense of togetherness, or smash a relationship apart. It can enrich a partnership, or turn the playground into a battlefield. Apart from sex, it is the only occupation which necessitates the two of you working together with immense goodwill and careful negotiation. 'Isn't it your turn to look after the baby?' 'Why is it always me who gets the smelly nappy?' And as the years go by it doesn't get any easier. 'Why did you tell him he could have the car tonight?' 'Why do you let her stay out so late?' 'Why do you never insist they wash the dishes?'

The minefield is made yet more tricky to negotiate by the knowledge that parenting is a fearfully dangerous pursuit, which may have lasting repercussions for future generations. On the other hand, I may simply be falling prey to the guilt neurosis of every mother. Still, when I think about fathers and daughters, or mother and sons, it seems to me that the riches my children will experience in their future relationships is almost commensurate with the measure of the wholeness of theirs with their father and me – and that's an altogether fearful, joyful and wonderful responsibility.

PARENTING TOGETHER

It is difficult for the husband when his wife has a baby. She gets all the attention while he is lucky if anyone notices him! He has to shoulder a lot more responsibility, give a lot of extra care and attention to his wife, help look after her and the baby when they come home from hospital, do a lot of household jobs he is not used to, cope with his wife's depression and tears, manage without sleep, and still go off to work every day. He may be in a state of nerves and shock, especially if he has been with his wife during a difficult labour. A sensitive man can be deeply upset to see the woman he loves in pain for several hours. What he needs most are a few quiet days and plenty of sleep and of course those are the last things he gets. He too needs help and support from his friends at church.

Jenny Cooke

Written in 1981 about not quite the new man. Youth worker Colin Phillimore from Lancaster, however, took a part-time job so that he could be completely involved in bringing up his son. He concurs with the helplessness men feel at seeing their wives in such pain, but he also writes lyrically about the sheer wonder of becoming a first-time father. 'I tend to write poems at times of great emotion, frequently at 2.00 a.m. in the morning when no other outward expression is sufficient to put across my feelings. Men generally have very few avenues to show their feelings and writing has always served as an acceptable replacement for my emotions. I do have some very dear friends who listen and accept me for being so open and I am now learning to be more public in challenging the traditional male role models that can be so damaging in men's personal development.

'The birth of our son on New Year's Eve was a powerful experience. The peace that we experienced that Christmas seemed to flow into my thoughts as I wrote, and "all was calm, all was bright" following a very distressing twenty-five-hour labour. It was difficult leaving mother and baby in hospital and returning to an empty house. I slept on various settees in the next five days as I refused to sleep in our bed until everyone was safely home. The only thing I could do to stop myself from exploding was to write a poem for each of us. Only then could I feast on a hearty pizza and a bottle of beer.'

The Mother

This was not how it was supposed to happen.
So strong, and fit and as ready as could be possible,
Taking everything in your stride,
So naturally, as naturally as the mother you are
Will be.

You dealt with everything so well,
For so long, so very long
And I am so proud.

And then what a change.
Total distress, total pain.
But to see you in peace and happy to be free of pain
Was special.
And then to see your face as our son is born,
Well, what words can do justice,
How do I vocalize my thoughts?

You did it.
All three of us did it.
But your bravery was astounding.
And now a-suckling,
We are complete, our lives fulfilled.
Born parents, fulfilling their purpose.
And all is calm, all is bright
Well done my strong one.

The Father

I shed my tears for you
My chest filling with distress, for my loved one is
    hurting.
I reached out, but could do nothing –
But stroke and hold your hand,
And kiss your forehead.
Such inadequacy, as you suffer so,
And I can do nothing.

The scene that still haunts me, metal on such frail
    flesh.
No majestic entrance to life, but a fight,
And yet listen to the calm that now invades us as
    he is born.

Our son and all is done.
It is finished and all is calm.
And we are together,
In peace, with our tender feelings for each other,
Together at last.

Colin Phillimore

If only it all continued as it began – mother, father and baby; peace, harmony and joy. But somehow the reality of daily survival takes over, and before you know it the wonder and mystery have gone. It's always fascinating to see how a man and a woman reorganize their relationship around their off-spring. Life is complex enough dealing with the arrival of one little bomb – but what about two? At one time the man simply got out of the way. Not any more. Total involvement from the moment of conception is the order of the day. This is Duncan Moore's experience:

'Wendy and I met in the dark, wet November of 1981 in that most romantic of settings: Milton Keynes. Neither of us at that time were involved with the church. We were married in August 1984 and within a couple of years had become committed Christians. As we both love children our thoughts turned towards having a family and we tried, unsuccessfully, for several years, to get ourselves pregnant. Incredibly, for a number of reasons, we divorced in 1990. Neither of us were truly happy and in 1991 we began courting anew. It meant going right back to the beginning, learning more about each other, and it led to our reconciliatory marriage in April 1992. Our prayers were finally answered in August 1994, when, after one previous and heartbreaking failed attempt, our second IVF treatment was successful and we fell pregnant. Our babies, India and Eden, born in April 1995, are true gifts from God, to whom we are eternally grateful.'

A Quick Trip Out

'It's a beautiful, warm, sunny morning. Let's take the
  kids out.'
'OK – you get them ready, I'll organize the rest.'
(Thinks) . . . so what do we need for a quick trip out?
'How long are we going for?'
'Oh, just a couple of hours.'
Right then, we'll need . . .
2 disposable nappies each
Plus 2 spare disposable nappies each
Nappy sack
Baby wipes
Cotton wool
Sunblock
2 bottles of baby milk
2 teats
2 spare teats
2 spare vests
2 spare pairs of socks *(no need to be excessive)*
Antiseptic cream
2 spare cardigans
1 spare dress
1 spare pair of dungarees
1 hat for a boy
1 hat for a girl
Double pack of kitchen roll
1 box of tissues
Pack of assorted bandages and sticking plasters
Video camera and spare batteries
35 mm SLR camera with wide angle and zoom
  facility
35 mm compact camera with flash facility
2 spare films

'Do we need the changing mat?'
'Yes.'
Changing mat
Sainsbury's plastic carrier bag
'What about the breast pump?'
'Yes.'
'And the steam sterilizer?'
'Yes.'
*'Had I better pack the twelve-metre extension lead
   then?'*
'Yes.'
Electric breast pump and ancillary equipment
Steam sterilizer
12 m extension lead
'Are you ready yet?'
'Yes, I think so.'
'Have you got the spare pram blankets?'
'No.'
'Spare pram sheets?'
'No.'
'Parasols?'
'No.'
'What on earth have you been doing all this time?'
4 spare pram blankets
4 spare pram sheets
2 parasols
'Are you ready now?'
'Yes, I think so.'
'OK, let's go.'
'Have you brought the washing in?
Don't forget to lock the back door.
Did you close the bathroom window?
You'd better set the alarm.
Nipple shields.'

'*Pardon?*'
'Did you remember to pack my nipple shields? You
  know I can't go anywhere without them.'
2 nipple shields
'*Right then . . . all packed up . . . let's go.*'
'We can't. It's raining.'

Duncan Moore

MOTHERS AND SONS

All women become like their mothers. That is their
tragedy. No man does. That's his.

Oscar Wilde (1854–1900)
The Importance of Being Earnest

The relationship between a man and his mother is arguably the
most important in his life. This first experience of woman can
lead him to love or hate, fear or enjoy the opposite sex. Deny
a man maternal intimacy at the early stage of his life and his
future relationships with both sexes may be thwarted. On the
other hand, a mother can indulge her son, especially if her
relationship with the father is disappointing or non-existent,
so that the son becomes the substitute man in her life. Even in
good mother-son relationships there must come a letting go on
the part of the mother, and a breaking free by the son, so that
he can form a lasting and meaningful relationship with his
partner. If he doesn't there may be rivalry and resentment
between the women in his life; confusion, tension and divided
loyalties in his. Small wonder a woman weighs up her prospective mother-in-law with interest, and even suspicion. She

knows that, good or bad, dead or alive, 'Mother' will always remain a powerful force for him.

Originally from South Africa, Dr Archibald Hart is the dean of the Graduate School of Psychology at the Fuller Theological Seminary in California. His book on male sexuality was written, he claims, after more than twenty-five years of meeting men he considered 'normal', many of them ministers of the church, who struggled nonetheless to come to terms with their sex drive.

The Roots of Male Sensuality

The male who lacks sensuality also lacks sensitivity and is unable to serve as a satisfactory sexual partner because he doesn't enjoy the broader experience of sex. If he isn't getting intercourse he isn't happy. He's never satisfied with anything less.

How does this come about? By depriving boys of the basic building blocks of sensuality – kissing, hugging, touching, stroking, being close to another. Those experiences are sensual because they have to do with our senses. They do not, of themselves, constitute anything sexual. But for sexuality to be sensual, a boy, and later a man, must feel comfortable with these basic building blocks. . . .

Women find it easier than men because while growing up they've been loved more overtly. We hug and kiss girls more than we do boys. But boys need hugging too. They need to be kissed by both parents. Physical contact of a nonsexual nature helps to open up sexual touching later.

Archibald Hart

Born of Austrian parents, journalist and poet Veronica Zundel grew up in Coventry. Her mother was Jewish. For several years she was assistant editor of the radical Christian magazine, Third Way, *often writing about singleness and the role of women in the church. She has compiled a number of anthologies including* Faith in Her Words, *a selection of poems by more than one hundred women poets, and her own poems have appeared in several volumes of poetry. In 1989, when she was thirty-six, she married Ed Sirett. Their son John, born when she was forty-one, has changed her life.*

A Prayer for Restraint

I am a hungry mother
I feed, feed on the sight of my child sleeping
his features blurred as a face in the floating womb.
I suck the sight of his flesh as he sucks
my tingling teats, my warm milk flowing.
I nibble his arm, his toes, sweet as a lover.

O I am a hungry mother; may my hunger
not devour my child, mine and not mine
O may my teeth not tear him, my treasure,
O may my starved heart swallowing not destroy him.

Veronica Zundel

Diane Tyers was born thirty-four years ago in the West Indies, but has lived in Britain for most of her life. She takes up the theme of letting her boys go at the next stage of their lives, when it begins to become a painful reality. Diane, who is married to Phil, vicar of St Matthew's in Preston, has three boys. She was a journalist before they were born, and is about to retrain as a teacher.

Bringing Up Boys

When I had my babies it didn't occur to me then they were male, in the full sense of the word. Of course I knew they were boys biologically, but the pure emotion of producing a child was the overriding force at the time. It is only now, faced with a fast-developing ten-year-old and his two younger brothers not far behind, that I am forced to stop in my tracks and acknowledge their manhood.

My gender-free little boys are taking on their masculine identity and are entering a world where I have little insight or even permission to enter. I can ease them through their pain and confusion of life, but I can never be a fellow sharer in their sexuality. I suppose I have reached the point where I see them disappearing, one by one, into the Locker Room, that place where all boys go through the rites of initiation, and I must let them go if they are to fulfil another important stage of their development.

The pregnancy, childbirth and breast-feeding part was my big gift to the boys. From it came the undeniable bonding between mother and child that affects body and soul. It is not a man's portion, but now I see the father-son dynamic bursting into life before my eyes. As I let go, my husband takes hold. Whatever the boys do or want to do, he has done; whatever they dream, he has dreamed; whatever agony of growing up they go through, he has gone through; whatever naughty act they commit, he has committed – and twice as badly! 'Yes,' he says to them, in one of their dialogues, 'I know just what you mean.'

It is a strange and necessary phenomenon as I see it. The dawning of their puberty and subsequent catapulting into life develops the hermetic father-son relationship to which no woman has the key.

Diane Tyers

And here is letting go from the son's perspective. Sometimes only death itself can fully sever the man from the little boy longing for the mother-son intimacy he once knew.

Russ Parker was raised in a very close-knit family in Birkenhead. A prolific writer and preacher on subjects such as dreams and the healing ministry, he is director of the Acorn Healing Trust.

Screaming in the Hospital

By the time I got to the hospital my mum was already in a coma. My brother Ray stared up at me from his seat: 'Why weren't you here earlier?' his eyes screamed at me. He sat beside her, brooding and silent. Lynn, my older sister, gave me a hug and said, 'It won't be long now.' I bent down and kissed Mum on the cheek, the believer inside me hoping she would miraculously wake up and smile. No such luck, no such faith! I looked down at the unfamiliar and repellent shape that was once my mum and cursed the doctors and nurses. A few days ago I had telephoned to see how she was. They told me she was doing fine. They sounded confident and in control and I thought I had time to get up there to say some proper goodbyes. It was Lynn's desperate call this morning that shattered and wounded me. 'You'd better get up here, quick, Russ, me mum looks like dying.'

Now all my anger stuck inside me and I felt like a little boy, powerless and helpless to save the day, rescue my mum, and get back to the way it was. It was then I realized, maybe too late, that I loved my mum and I would miss her and nobody would take my pain away. Not even Jesus who I know is acquainted with grief. 'Why the bloody hell do people have to die like Jesus?' I hissed under my breath, but carefully, so that my brothers and sisters wouldn't see my Christian confidence falling down like loose underwear.

Russ Parker

FATHERS AND DAUGHTERS

If boys depend on their mothers to teach them the value of sensitivity and intimacy, girls need their fathers to affirm their femininity and desirability. A man who takes pride in his daughter gives her an invaluable gift: a sense of beauty and self-worth. But sadly the best gifts are always open to abuse, and this has laid a terrible burden on men as they struggle with the way their natural, fatherly instincts, and normal longing for appropriate physical contact, which a daughter needs, can now be deemed sinister and unacceptable.

But when the relationship between a man and his daughter is at its best it can be one of the most rewarding, tender, liberating experiences for woman – even if the man is not the natural father.

Revd Maureen Witcombe (Mo) was the Bishop of Sheffield's advisor on women's ministry, and one of the first women in this country to be priested. She now lives in Uxbridge, where her husband, John, is vicar of St Margaret's. They have three children.

Mo's real mother became desperately ill when Mo was only a baby. Her father, who already had an older child to care for, couldn't cope with a baby as well, and asked his wife's sister and her husband, who were childless, whether they would be prepared to look after her. Mo's real mother died three years later.

The phone rang. It was a crackly line from Hastings.

'I'm bringing the baby home.'

Henny Penny (his real name was Henry), immediately set about finding a cot, and all the other things they would need before his wife arrived with the baby at Liverpool's Lime Street Station the following day. There was no debate, or discussion. He accepted me with love and joy from the very first moment he saw me.

We were always close. At times, inseparable. Some of my earliest memories are helping him by digging up the precious plants I thought were weeds down on his allotment. He was a teacher and I accompanied him to school every day. Each morning playtime I walked down the long corridor to his classroom for my peeled apple. He could also be a source of embarrassment as he had the loudest voice in the school.

By this time I had been legally adopted and Henny Penny had become Daddy. I was without doubt a 'Daddy's Girl'. We did the Saturday morning shop together. We cooked the tea together and sneaked a book on to the table to read at mealtimes when my mother was out at work. He took me to Brownies, ballet, singing lessons and was always there to pick me up if it was dark. When Brownies was late, he wanted to know why.

My father had great hopes for me. I don't think there was anything he thought I couldn't do because of my gender. The household chores were fairly evenly distributed. There was little sexism in our house.

I knew how much he loved me and it is from him that I learned the richness there can be in male-female relationships. When I was a child I used to watch him ensconced in his large, comfortable Parker Knoll armchair, reading his usual Western, and I remember being overcome by a sense of his mortality, and almost paralysed with fear at the thought of losing him. I pushed the idea out of my mind.

We had years together. Yet he died of lung cancer when I was only seventeen, and I was completely devastated.

I have now lived longer without him, then with him. The memory of his presence still aches within me, but because of it I have no fear of men, especially men in authority. I don't expect to be treated badly, or as a lesser mortal, just because I am a woman. My father never did, so why should anyone else? I enjoy male company and friendship. That was his bequest to me, along with a deeper understanding of how God fathers his precious daughter.

Mo Witcombe

Some men will not be able to identify with the following experience, but it is an interesting example of how differently men and women can approach the same situation. One clergyman describes how he and his wife took their daughter's decision to give her baby away. The paternal instinct arouses in him a fierce protectiveness for his little girl. The maternal instinct takes his wife down a totally different path.

When Jacky became pregnant at sixteen she was mature enough to know she wasn't old enough to handle marriage, or bringing up a child. At the same time she knew she could never go through an abortion, and opted instead for adoption. All I wanted was for my little girl to survive the trauma with the minimum pain and scarring, which she did. We're a close family and the crisis brought us closer than ever. What I never counted on was my wife's reaction. She only wanted the best for our daughter too, but how she grieved for the grandson she lost. Every January 31 she says, 'He'll be five today' or 'He'll be six today.' For her the baby was a real person, whereas as far as I'm concerned I never had a grandson. I have no sense of loss whatsoever in that respect.

Thinking about it, I suppose it's very similar to becoming a father. When my wife was pregnant I remember escorting her everywhere with such a sense of pride, lowering her into chairs at restaurants, thinking, 'This is all my doing, this is.' But I only really became a father the day my daughter was born and I could see, and fall in love with actual flesh and blood.

But what if the 'falling in love' is parodied and distorted? When a daughter is denied an appropriate male presence, when her rights and trust are abused, the consequences are destructive and lasting, as this poem by Stewart Henderson states so baldly.

I Don't Like Men

I don't like men
they're loud and rather coarse
they have a funny smell
I much prefer a horse

I don't like men
they think they're always right
that's such a weight to bear
when they're really not that bright

I don't like men
they leave me rather numb
A consequence of meeting
the emotionally dumb

I don't like men
yet when I air this view
some women shout me down
I wonder why they do?

I don't like men
my maiden's bubble burst
I can't lie down and love
as my daddy got there first

I don't like men
It's better with Yvonne
It's probably my fault
I must have led him on.

Stewart Henderson

Even the appropriate 'falling in love' of a man with his daugh-ter has to be carefully worked out, especially as she grows older. My husband was very taken aback when our thirteen-year-old daughter suddenly said to him one day, 'Dad, you really will have to stop patting my bum.' He simply hadn't given a thought to the implications of such an affectionate gesture. Accepting her wishes, bowing to her adulthood, releasing her from the safe and cosy niche she has created in his heart, is all part of that vital letting go, required of a father, as much as of a mother.

John Stickley is first and foremost an actor and a writer. He was a businessman, but in 1991 when his business 'disappeared down the toilet', he found himself in the midst of a huge

personal crisis, struggling to find out who he was, what was of
value in his life and whether God and more especially, institu-
tional religion had any part to play.

I was talking to a friend of mine in the street and something across the road caught my eye. It is no use denying
that I have a refined ability to spot a pretty woman in my
peripheral vision while undertaking any other activity,
and this was such a time. In a microsecond I had glimpsed
long blond hair flowing as she walked, tight jeans, slightly
faded over the seat of her pert bottom and confidence in
her walk. I did a 'double take' to get a better view of her
beauty.

Then realized it was my fourteen-year-old daughter.

It was the first time I had seen her like that and there
then followed a few confused seconds of astonishment,
unbelief, guilt, joy, pride and a sense of my mortality as I
watched her walk up the street.

Until she was born I had not known (how could I) that
I had a daughter-shaped hole at the centre of my being
that only she could fill. Now she is a young woman and
a very good friend, my flesh and blood, who will one day
bear my grandchild.

And she does have a lovely bottom.

John Stickley

LOSING A CHILD

My wife was treated as having lost someone she loved. I was being treated as having lost someone I was responsible for. I felt like shouting, 'I loved him too you know.'

They Were Our Children Too, Grief of Fathers
Bereaved by a Cot Death

What if a child, so loved and longed-for, dies? How do men and women respond to that greatest sorrow of all? Everyone rallies around the mother, empathizes with her in her grief and despair. But what of the father's needs? 'How is your wife?' his friends tend to say. Officials tend to see it as his job to register the death, make the funeral arrangements, provide the basic information, make the decisions, reinforcing the idea that women can go to pieces, but men have to be strong, stay in control.

At no time in his life, perhaps, is it harder to be a man. But what does being a man in this situation really mean?

Marion Pitman won the 1985 Christian Poetry Competition. Her poems, which often confront the polite and superficial way we keep our distance from each other, have been published in various collections. She lives in Twickenham where she keeps a second-hand book and bric-a-brac shop, and is assistant editor of Collectors Mart. *She has no children of her own.*

Hero

and when he died his mother's grief was public show
replete with public sympathy
His father, locked in his private room
cried out his broken heart alone
till he had no tears left

then went out dry-eyed
How brave his father is they said How brave.

Marion Pitman

But every now and then, a man finds the courage to force his way against the flow and 'go public' with his pain. And it seems in some extraordinary way that he is most truly himself when, like the God in whose image he was made, he is in touch with his feelings.

Phil and Linda Henry had already experienced one miscarriage when Linda became pregnant with Charlie. To all intents and purposes this was a perfectly normal pregnancy – until the thirty-sixth week. For reasons no one could explain Charlie died in the uterus and Linda had to give birth to a stillborn baby. Just over a year later, on 29 January 1995, Phil got up to describe in our church what the last few months had been like for him. This is what he said:

I'm sorry it's taken me so long to get round to sharing this with you. I just wanted to be able to get all the way through without bursting into floods of tears. Not because of any embarrassment, but because I want to tell you the whole story. I'm still not sure even now that I'll manage it – so apologies in advance in case I suddenly have to flee before I finish.

When Charlie died we were left not only with our grief, but with a host of doubts, of questions like, 'Why me?' and 'What is suffering for?' and we discovered that there are no easy answers. Above all there was the intense pain, almost unbearable at times. Even now, over a year later, I still feel bad some of the time, still miss him terribly and feel very weak and incapable. But slowly I'm becoming aware that we are much stronger than before, and we cope much better than before with many things. Our faith is in fact stronger. In some strange, almost indescribable way I feel more alive. I seem to experience life rather than just passing through it. It still hurts, but at the same time, in some strange, almost inexplicable way, the sun seems brighter, the grass greener.

I have often thanked God for all the people who were so understanding and helpful, but I've never felt able to thank those people in person, so here we are. THANK YOU. Thanks for the cards, flowers, letters. They were a great comfort to us. Thank you especially for praying – we couldn't have coped without that.

It says in Matthew's Gospel, 'And about the ninth hour Jesus cried with a loud voice, saying, "Eli, Eli, lama sabachthani?" that is to say, "My God, my God, why have you forsaken me?" The cry of a son abandoned by his father. I often used to think about that from Christ's point of view, but rarely from the father's angle. Now though, I find it especially poignant. God the Father willingly sacrificed his only son for us. Just think on that for a moment. I have lost a son whom I hardly knew. I had felt him kick and heard his heartbeat. When he died it just about broke my heart. How much more must it have hurt God to lose his son with whom he has a perfect relationship? And he did it willingly for us.

3

Like Brother and Sister

The relationship between siblings when one is male and one female can bring out the best in boys: their protectiveness, sensitivity, love and generosity. Yet it may not last.

I feel very wistful as I read George Eliot's account of sibling love. All kinds of delightful memories come flooding back of my own two children in their early years, thoroughly enjoying each other's company, each other's gender, he holding her hand, guiding and guarding, she gazing up at him with love, trust and pride.

Our Joel was three and a half when his sister was born. 'I so much wanted the little creature to talk back to me', he said, 'and when she started communicating, using words I could recognize, I was so excited. I remember her sitting on the rocks, her swimming costume all wrinkled because she'd no waist. She was so cute.' And all was well while she remained little, malleable and weak. But one day, before we noticed it, she became her own woman and rejected his protectiveness and pedantry. Equality was what she wanted, and he couldn't cope with it. How could the little girl with cherubic face and golden curls, whose dependency had made him feel a giant, suddenly grow to be his size? How could she know all he knew, walk through the world without him? 'Growing up ruins everything', he says. She says, 'If only he didn't have to prove how tough he was in front of his friends. He points out the mistakes I make that no one else has noticed.' How is it possible that adoration could turn to such irritation?

The story of all men and women is there. For two teenagers, loving is no longer automatic. Now they have to work at it. He is learning that she has strengths. She is learning that he has fears. They're both learning they can still walk together, but with a little more distance between them. Much of his pride in her feminine attractions, much of her enjoyment of his boisterous male energy, returns at unguarded moments, enough I hope to provide them with a foundation for the future, for their and many other cross-gender relationships. 'I envy my friend, Pete, who has four brothers all going to Greenbelt together', says Joel. 'But on the other hand, having a sister does bring a very different, and very special dimension into my life.'

The nineteenth-century novelist George Eliot, whose real name was Mary Ann Evans, grew up adoring her brother, the inspiration for Tom in The Mill on the Floss. *But she deeply upset him, when, as an adult, she turned away from the severe Calvinism of her teens, flagrantly defied the social norm, and set up home with the married writer George Henry Lewes. Throughout her 24-year relationship with Lewes, her brother refused all contact with her, picking up the threads only after Lewes' death. There is a moral to the story. There always is with broken relationships. It may be too late to repair them. George Eliot died within months of finding her brother again.*

from **Brother and Sister**

I.
I cannot choose but think upon the time
When our two lives grew like two buds that kiss

At lightest thrill from the bee's swinging chime,
Because the one so near the other is.

He was the elder and a little man
Of forty inches, bound to show no dread,
And I the girl that puppy-like now ran,
Now lagged behind my brother's larger tread.

I held him wise, and when he talked to me
Of snakes and birds, and which God loved the best,
I thought his knowledge marked the boundary
Where men grew blind, though angels knew the rest.

If he said 'Hush!' I tried to hold my breath;
Wherever he said 'Come!' I stepped in faith.

9.
We had the self-same world enlarged for each
By loving difference of girl and boy:
The fruit that hung on high beyond my reach
He plucked for me, and oft he must employ

A measuring glance to guide my tiny shoe
Where lay firm stepping-stones, or call to mind
'This thing I like my sister may not do,
For she is little, and I must be kind'.

Thus boyish Will the nobler mastery learned
Where inward vision over impulse reigns,
Widening its life with separate life discerned,
A Like unlike, a Self that self restrains.

His years with other must the sweeter be
For those brief days he spent in loving me.

10.

School parted us; we never found again
That childish world where our two spirits mingled
Like scents from varying roses that remain
One sweetness, nor can evermore be singled.

Yet the twin habit of that early time
Lingered for long about the heart and tongue:
We had been natives of one happy clime
And its dear accent to our utterance clung.

Till the dire years whose awful name is Change
Had grasped our souls still yearning in divorce,
And pitiless shaped them in two forms that range
To elements which sever their life's course.

But were another childhood-world my share,
I would be born a little sister there.

George Eliot

On the other hand, the relationship can be a potential for disaster. Swiss psychologist Paul Tournier believed that male scorn, be it from a father or a brother, can do women a great deal of lasting damage.

Boys make fun of girls, especially on the approach of adolescence, when desire is awakening, though it is not yet ready to express itself openly, and so is hidden under sarcastic remarks. An attractive woman may doubt her seductive powers all her life because a brother was once in the habit of referring to her as an ugly duckling, so that she never discovers the make-up or hair-style which suits her, and even thinks men are looking at her with contempt when their glances are in fact prompted by desire. Another imposes a fiendishly strict diet upon herself in order to slim, simply because her brother used to call her Fatty.

Christianity proclaims that the despised are blessed . . . but society remains full of prejudices, and the one about male superiority persists despite all the concessions made to feminism. Women themselves more often than not believe themselves to be inferior . . . Our society, like our own hearts, puts masculine values first: success, prestige. We sing of love among men, but go on competing against each other, trying to outshine each other, to triumph over each other. And in order to get themselves accepted as equals women have to play the same dangerous game.

Paul Tournier

Some men, like Mary Slessor's brother Robert, seem to be convinced of an innate male superiority from an early age. The irony, in the following piece, is that Mary Slessor turned out to be one of the greatest missionaries who ever lived. Born in 1848, the daughter of an alcoholic father and devout, hard-working mother, Mary worked as a weaver in a Dundee mill from the age of eleven. She went to the African Calabar in 1876 and such was her influence in eradicating human sacrifice and drunkenness that 'The Great White Ma' as she was known, was made Vice-Consul of the Calabar by the British Colonial Service.

'You're only a Girl'

She was very good at make-believe, and one of her games was to sit in a corner and pretend that she was keeping school. If you had listened to her you would have found the pupils she was busy teaching and keeping in order were children with skins as black as coal. The reason was this. Her mother took a great interest in all she heard on Sundays about the dark lands beyond the sea where millions of people had never heard of Jesus. The church to which she belonged had sent out many brave men and women to various parts of the world to fight the evils of heathenism, and a new Mission had just begun amongst a savage race in a wild country called Calabar in West Africa, and everyone in Scotland was talking about it and the perils and hardships of the missionaries. Mrs Slessor used to come home with all the news about the work, and the children would gather about her knees and listen to stories of the strange cruel customs of the natives, and how they killed twin-babies, until their eyes grew big and round, and their hearts raced with fear, and they snuggled close to her side.

Mary was very sorry for these helpless bush-children, and often thought about them, and that was why she made them her play scholars. She dreamed, too, of going out some day to that terrible land and saving the lives of the 'twinnies', and sometimes she would look up and say: 'Mother, I want to be a missionary and go out and teach the black boys and girls real ways.'

Then Robert would retort in the tone boys often use with their sisters: 'But you're only a girl, and girls can't be missionaries. *I'm* going to be one and you can come out with me, and if you're good I may let you up into my pulpit beside me.'

Notice the proprietorial 'my' pulpit, and the gracious, 'I may let you'. But times have changed – a little. When I read this piece to my fourteen-year-old daughter Abby she said, 'And what happened to Robert? Did he end up selling double glazing?' She believes men don't live up to their boasts, while women aren't foolish enough to boast in the first place. To be fair to Robert Slessor, it is still difficult in our family to adjust to the idea that Abby now has as much right to be a vicar one day as her elder brother.

When Veronica Zundel's elder brother committed suicide at the age of twenty-seven in 1975, she was left to come to terms with the immense void he left behind.

Ballad of the Brotherless

He was my brother
of my own blood
now he is gone over
alone I stand guard

Now he is gone over
to the far shore
alone I stand guard
on a bare spur

I cannot tell
if he rest or burn
into God's turning hand
God grant he turn

Friends I have many
beside me to stand
but none of my own blood
none of my land

Friends I have many
trusted and true
but none of my own blood
to pay blood's due

He was my brother
troubled sore
God speed his boat gentle
to thy far shore

Veronica Zundel

4

We're Just Good Friends

This is the era when everyone seems to ask, 'Can men and women ever be friends without sex getting in the way?' Up until the last war no one ever considered the question. Social etiquette kept the sexes strictly segregated. But our new freedom, for all its advantages, has left us feeling a little bewildered. Many of the people I interviewed were certain that deep platonic love between a man and a woman must be a possibility – until they thought about it at length. They longed for it, but few had in fact experienced it, except perhaps when they were single.

The problem is how does one go about finding it? It is normal and acceptable to lunch with a work colleague, though even that has its risks. But how can you call on your friend's husband, or wife, and ask them out for a drink or to go to the cinema? Whether you are married or single the chances are they will misread the signs. And if they don't, everyone else will. I have few male friends other than sharing my husband's, or sharing the husbands of my female friends. And that fills me with a certain regret, for I enjoy male company and a male perspective on a situation is often different from a woman's. There's no doubt that men open themselves up to women more easily than to other men. That does of course have its pitfalls too, but where is the relationship without risk?

And once you have real cross-gender friendship, how do you preserve and nurture it? One woman told me that she and a male friend had become very close leading a church home group together – until he had become aggressive, threatened by her competence. Another described the way a friendship with a man had blossomed, until his wife became bitter and jealous. Both said they would never explore such a friendship again.

Dr Archibald Hart believes that men and women live on such different planets that friendship is almost out of the question. But then his view may be affected by the time he spends counselling men with sexual problems. Catholic priest Ronald Rolheiser on the other hand feels that the church has become infected by society's confusion between sexuality and the sex act, losing a potential life-enhancing resource. But he is celibate, and motivated by the need to establish non-genital relationships with women. So is one or both, or neither of them, right?

It is not without significance that this is the shortest section in the book. If deep, pure and lasting friendship is possible between a man and a woman, where is it? Perhaps it is a special gift from God reserved for the single. Theologian and priest, Henri Nouwen, describing the work of his friend Jean Vanier with mentally handicapped people, has this challenge for us all. He says, 'Men and women who are often not able to develop sexual relationships teach us most about true intimacy.'

Platonic love, or friendship can be easily misread by males. A woman, for instance, might think that only a friendship is developing, perhaps with a male acquaintance at work. She enjoys doing things with him. She knows the boundaries. They laugh, share stories, and have lunch. For her it is all platonic, pure friendship. There's no love, so there can't possibly be anything sexual . . . .

The man, oblivious to his deeper feelings, only thinks with his hormones. 'She's interested in sex', he thinks. 'She's got to be. Why else would she be so friendly?' Is he right? Not at all. And if he tries to take it further he could be in serious trouble.

Men and women view the link between love and sex differently. But instead of making sex simpler for men, this differences makes it more complex. Men don't have an innate defence against sexual arousal, so they have to construct it for themselves. Not many men are effective in creating this protection, so ladies beware. Men don't always do a good job of being 'just friends' with a woman.

Archibald Hart

Perhaps there needs to be a clear declaration of intent right from the beginning. But who is going to be the first to say, 'Of course you realize that this is just friendship', without causing deep affront to the other, whose motives were entirely pure anyway? If our only solution is to make such relationships taboo, aren't we in danger of closing the door on an invaluable opportunity for men to find the self-confidence which the friendship of women can give them?

A man needs to feel very deeply loved in order to share an intimate secret charged with emotion. Thus he may relate a strange experience which happened one day, and which was for him a mysterious intervention of God in his life. He may tell of some dreamlike ideal to which he holds very deeply. Again, he may tell of an inner call, a sense of mission which he is to fulfil in this world. It seemed to him that he could never dare speak of it to another. He feared that it would appear ridiculous and vain. And yet, suddenly, without his knowing why, the rapport with another has become such that he uncovers his long-hidden secret.

Deep sharing is overwhelming, and very rare. A thousand fears keep us in check. First of all there is the fear of breaking down, of crying. There is especially the fear that the other will not sense the tremendous importance with which this memory or feeling is charged. How difficult it is when such a difficult sharing falls flat, upon ears that do not sense the significance of what we're saying.

Paul Tournier

If a man shares his deepest longings with a woman other than his wife, how do they avoid the pitfalls and maintain their integrity? This is Sue, a single woman priest, talking about her relationship with a married male priest and close colleague.

Is ours a working relationship or a friendship? Both, I suppose and that means walking a tightrope. If you're both determined to be ruthlessly honest with each other and keep short accounts, it can be done. It's about very basic things like knowing when the hug has to stop. I can tell. I may want it to go a while longer. I may feel I need it. But discipline has to take over. If you really love each other, you respect each other. If we messed around we'd lose the most important thing in our relationship: Jesus. And then what good would we be to anyone else? The very reason for our relationship would go and we would have nothing left.

The real danger comes if he is a man whose sexuality is wrapped up in dependency, if he needs lots of feminine adulation, if he needs intimacy, if he's looking for mother. It's flattering when a man finds you attractive, but beware, you can be sucked into that big black hole in the centre of his being. And so will every other woman he meets.

The relationship has to be on a level if there is to be mutual love and safety. Being friends with his spouse really helps. But there's no way round it. If you are going to be close, it isn't going to be easy.

There is no escaping our sexuality. It influences all our relationships. A chemistry is at work in same-sex friendships, as well as in friendships between the sexes. That's why friendship is such a tender, precious plant, requiring careful nurturing. Roman Catholic priest, Ronald Rolheiser, Vice Dean of Theology at Newman Theological College, Edmonton, Canada, writes, 'Few things are as healing and life-giving as is friendship between woman and man. . . . But it is rare. Deep, intimate, chaste heterosexual friendship is no small achievement. It requires a delicate balance between caution and risk, between inhibition and daring vulnerability. But it is worth the risk and effort.'

For all kinds of reasons we cannot sleep with everyone we feel drawn to and since friendship and love become too much linked to sex we are constantly torn between infidelity and frustration. . . .

49

It is no accident that in our culture it is easier to find a lover than a friend, just as it is no accident that, in our culture, virginity, celibacy, chastity within deep friendships and periodic abstinence within marriage are considered to be unrealistic or even positively harmful. Yet our deepest hungers and longings are for heterosexual relations beyond having sex. The ache is for men and women to come together as more than lovers. . . . Physically, psychologically, spiritually, emotionally, intellectually and aesthetically we ache for union with something beyond ourselves. Maleness aches for femaleness, femaleness for the male. Sex colours all. Yet having sex is merely one specific expression of our sexuality. . . .

There is a sex of the groin and sex of the heart. The former is full of dissatisfaction, exploitation, superficiality, schizophrenia and ultimately, boredom. The latter is full of friendship, romance and passion. It is the sex of the heart that cures loneliness and creates family, community and friendship.

Ronald Rolheiser

5

Love Makes the World Go Round

There are four things that are too mysterious for me
to understand:
    an eagle flying in the sky,
    a snake moving on a rock,
        a ship finding its way over the sea,
            and a man and a woman falling in love.

Proverbs 30.18 (Good News Bible)

My dear Sir.
This letter comes to know whether you will be pleased
to give me leave to propose marriage to your daughter,
Miss Elizabeth. You need not be afraid of sending me a
refusal; for I bless God, if I know anything of my own
heart, I am free from that foolish passion which the world
calls love.

George Whitefield, preacher (1714–70)

Whitefield to the father of his intended, Elizabeth, who was
ten years his senior, a widow and had neither fortune nor
beauty. She said yes, the mad fool! That is not to say that

arranged marriages, relationships which begin with the head rather than the heart, do not work. Indeed, many, including that doyen of emotional well-being, Scott Peck, believe that the high expectation of romantic love in our society has driven out other vital prerequisites for a happy relationship, such as loyalty, commitment, respect, selflessness, tenderness and good old not-so-common kindness. But where is the harm, Mr Whitefield, in a bit of sparkle too? Is all passion foolish, or just terribly un-English? Doesn't the God who gave his children one of the greatest love songs ever written, the Song of Songs, expect them to know the crazy, dizzying heights of emotion triggered by the magical chemistry between a man and a woman? Even if it may also mean plumbing the depths of despair. For without the ability to love, human beings would merely be yet another species within the animal kingdom. And real loving hurts, though the hurt is never wasted.

All the writers in this section agree that falling in love changes people, on the whole for the better. It makes them wiser, gentler, more giving, more accepting, of themselves as well as of the other. It enriches and adds colour to our lives, so that whether it continues as a burning spark at the heart of a mature relationship, or whether it is finally and sadly extinguished, it can remain a source of deep joy and thankfulness for those to whom the gift is given.

Women are vulnerable when we love, exposing ourselves as we do to the pain of rejection, but somehow men are more so. They're not allowed to fail. Their competitive streak and fragile ego won't allow it. Since the stakes are higher, there's more to lose.

Clive Price was, until 1994, the editor of Parentwise Magazine, *but is now working as a freelance journalist. He admits that to this day he still finds women a bit of a mystery. 'Their*

sexuality is so sophisticated, so . . . hidden.' Perhaps this first,
exquisitely painful experience of puppy love was to blame.

Playground Love

Exciting split-second glances
Across the classroom stupor
As teacher erases algebra
With the speed of an arthritic window cleaner.
Then, opening doors for
The one who has captured your affection;
Dodging sawdust piles in the corridor
Into the freedom of playtime.

You cram eternity into fifteen minutes
Hoping love will linger
By the gnarled old crab apple tree
Or behind the grotty bikesheds –
You catch a quick cheeky kiss
Like the first butterfly of summer.

Heaven has come to school.
She is everything to you,
With her curled-up exercise books
Tooth-bitten pencils
Textbook covers that say
'Marc Bolan is ACE'.
Her dad is getting ahead at the brewery
Her mum is a white collar worker
In the shirt factory.

You make a date –
Sunday afternoon in the park

Secret rendezvous
No one knows except your mother
'Cause you want to get back for tea
It's fish fingers and chips.

You wait by the park gates
Your heart is pounding inside your neck
You cannot
Wait
But you do
Wait
And
Wait

The crowds grow thinner
A small man buries dead leaves in his sack
The ice cream van belches smoke and drives away
But still you
Wait
Until dusk strokes the treetops
You kick a stone
You want to kick yourself
Stupid
Frustrated
Angry
Why? Why? Why?

You had it all planned
Now she has plans with another
(And you'd like to smash his head in, but he's bigger
    than you)
Your heart has a leaky valve
it strains to show a beat
You want to kick yourself

Stupid
Frustrated
Angry
Playground love.

Clive Price

On Falling in Love

Approach it properly
don't go daft over lipstick
or the way the body shapes itself in certain places
Refrain from finding your belle
then imagining her
bikini clad with seductive lips
offering you a martini
on an isolated beach in the Caribbean
this is known as fantasy
which is famous for its short term attractions
and will cause you to go out
and find another advert
Fall in love with the person
the skin, the teeth, the hair
get to know her giggle
the way she holds a cup of coffee
Love without walls
Approach it properly.

Stewart Henderson

*One of my earliest memories of going to the synagogue when
I was a teenager, and indeed, one of the advantages of sitting
in a gallery, is ogling the talent below. Years later, in a Free*

Church, I well remember the delights of peeping over the top of my hymnbook at the object of my admiration and desire on the other side of the congregation. How delicious, at least once in a lifetime, to be distracted from one's prayers by another, more earthly kind of worship.

Thomas Hardy (1840–1928), was a poet and author of seventeen novels, including Far from the Madding Crowd, Tess of the D'Urbervilles *and* Jude the Obscure, *set in a part of rural England he called 'Wessex'. As an ecclesiastical architect by training, he always had a particular love for old country churches, and for the many tender, human secrets to which they bore silent testimony down through the centuries.*

A Church Romance

She turned in the high pew, until her sight
Swept the west gallery, and caught its row
Of music-men with viol, book and bow
Against the sinking sad tower-window light.

She turned again; and in her pride's despite
One strenuous viol's inspirer seemed to throw
A message from his string to her below,
Which said: 'I claim thee as my own forthright!'

Thus their hearts' bond began, in due time signed.
And long years thence, when Age had scared Romance,
At some old attitude or glance

That gallery-scene would break upon her mind,
With him as minstrel, ardent, young and trim,
Bowing 'New Sabbath' or 'Mount Ephraim'.

Thomas Hardy

What is the secret ingredient in a relationship that suddenly, unintentionally turns friendship into love, transforming a quiet, tranquil walk on an even plain into a trip on a roller coaster? And is it wise to take the risk of teetering on the edge of the abyss? By contrast with preacher Whitefield's measured approach to passion, actor, impresario, songwriter and poet, Noel Coward (1899–1973), whose sexuality was what the Archbishop of York might call 'a grey area' decides that it is. Perhaps it is his very ambivalence which enables this most 'English' of men to articulate such a wealth of feeling.

I Knew You Once Without Enchantment

I knew you once without enchantment
And for some years
We went our usual ways
Meeting occasionally
Finding no heights nor depths among our days
Shedding no tears
Every so often when we felt inclined
Living like lovers in each other arms
Feeling no qualms
In our light intimacy
So resolute we were in heart and mind
So steeled against illusion, deaf and blind
To all presentiment, to all enchantment
(I knew you once without enchantment).

It is so strange
Remembering that phase
Those unexacting, uneventful days
Before the change
Before we knew this serio-comic, tragic

Most unexpected, overwhelming magic,
I knew you once without enchantment.

And today I cannot think of you without my heart
Suddenly stopping
Or, in those long grey hours we spent apart
Dropping, dropping
Down into desolation like a stone.
To be alone
No longer means to me clear time and space
Into which to stretch my mind.

I see your face
Between me and the space I used to find
Between me and the other worlds I seek
There stands your sleek
And most beloved silhouette
And yet
I can remember not so long ago

We neither of us cared
Nor dared
To know
How swiftly we were nearing the abyss
(This foolish, quite ungovernable bliss)
Let's not regret
That empty life before. It was great fun
And hurt no one
There was no harm in it
At certain moments there was even charm in it.

But oh my dearest love, there was no spell
No singing heaven and no wailing hell.
I knew you once without enchantment.

Noel Coward

*To many, 'enchantment' doesn't come as easily as it does in the
story books. Teacher Sue Bell of Lancaster never felt complete
as a single person. She always believed God had a knight in
shining armour for her. But as the years passed by, where was
he? And would the man of her dreams be all she hoped? She
and her husband, Tony, were put in touch with each other by
a Christian dating agency. But once the initial introduction
was made, what followed was a miracle, rather than a foregone
conclusion, and proof that the seeds of romantic love can be
carefully nurtured, rather than sprouting of their own accord.*

He'll Be Worth It when He Comes

'He'll be worth it when he comes', said a friend, as we
walked in the sunshine, discussing whether God could get
his timing wrong. She was one of a few people who had
loyally hung on to the vision that I would get married one
day. But I seemed to have been waiting an awful long
time. Here I was approaching my mid-thirties, and no
sign of any handsome prince.

Six months later he walked into my life. And did I rush
round in a state of blissful excitement sharing my joy
with everyone? No, I ran in the opposite direction.

I had always dreamed that I would know he was the
one the moment he appeared. But now that he had, I
couldn't quite believe it. This was flesh and blood, a real
man with thoughts, feelings, a mind of his own, a sense of
humour, not some romantic figment of my imagination.
God was answering my prayer. And it was scary. I was in
uncharted waters, and for once I wanted to cling to the
safe haven of my singleness, rather than give myself to a
stranger.

Slowly, with God's encouragment, and Tony's patience,

I began to admit to myself that I was falling in love. Learning to trust someone, listening to their opinions, accepting that I didn't have to stand on my own two feet all the time, hasn't been easy. I balked when I discovered he had better taste in choosing the colours for the decor of our home, when I first came in from work and found him doing the ironing.

We've been married for two years now, and has he been worth waiting for? He makes me laugh, listens to me, cooks the meals, does the housework, brings me flowers, massages my back during pregnancy. There's no one else on earth with whom I feel more comfortable. It's wonderful to be able to share my life with someone else. That was what I waited for in a man. And I haven't been disappointed.

Sue Bell

When a man and a woman are truly in love, it can potentially be God's way of providing each other with the antidote to insecurity. And even if it die one day, nothing takes away what once was.

Jean Clark, now in her late sixties, calls herself, like so many women, 'a late developer'. After twenty years as a wife and mother she became head of a polytechnic counselling service for students in Leicester, and a voluntary lay chaplain to students on the East Midlands Training Course for the Church of England ministry. Her marriage finally came to an end in 1985 and she moved to Norwich where she works as a freelance counsellor. She began to write poetry as a way of coming to terms with the deep and painful feelings that a broken marriage can create. And it is within that context that she looks back and remembers with thankfulness what two people once meant to each other.

A Kind of Loving

There was a beauty in our loving
that transfigured two plain people
into creatures filled with power
to love as lovers truly must

There was a tenderness in our loving
that oh, so gently held the other's pain
and sought, through honest words
to find the gritty grains of truth

There was an honour in our loving
that steadfastly denied
politeness or the holding back of truth
that even in the utter pain of loss
held us and set us free

Jean Clark

*Some, it seems, may wait in vain. Wendy Cope has become one
of Britain's most popular poets, loved for her funny, subversive
style. After taking her degree at St Hilda's College, Oxford, she
worked for fifteen years as a primary school teacher in London.
Her first collection of poems,* Making Cocoa for Kingsley Amis,
published in 1986, was the unpredicted literary hit of its year.

Bloody Men

Bloody men are like bloody buses –
You wait for one for about a year
And as soon as one approaches your stop
Two or three others appear.

You look at them flashing their indicators,
Offering you a ride.
You're trying to read the destinations,
You haven't much time to decide.

If you make a mistake, there's no turning back.
Jump off, and you'll stand there and gaze
While the cars and the taxis and lorries go by
And the minutes, the hours, the days.

Wendy Cope

6

Horse and Carriage

Rejoice in the wife of your youth,
a lovely deer, a graceful doe.
May her breasts satisfy you at all times;
May you be intoxicated always by her love.

Proverbs 5.18, 19 (New Revised Standard Version)

Ah, dear God, marriage is not a thing of nature but a gift of God, the sweetest, the dearest, and the purest life above all celibacy and all singleness, when it turns out well, though the very devil if it does not. For although women have the art with tears, lies and snares to beguile a man, they can also be superb and say the very best. If then these three remain in marriage – fidelity and faith, children and progeny, and the sacrament – it is to be considered a wholly divine estate.

Martin Luther

For whoever doesn't believe God has a sense of humour, I have but one word: marriage. What propels two human beings into sharing their peculiar habits and dirty laundry? Luther raised its status in society after centuries of belief that only lesser mortals succumbed to its lure, while the strong and sane remained single. But even he wondered how the patriarchs coped with six hundred years of it. Imagine being Abraham in old age, caught in the crossfire between two jealous women. Or Isaac, with nothing to listen to except the wrangling of Rebecca with Esau's wives. Luther fails to wonder how Sarah or Rebecca coped with their singularly short-sighted, unresponsive men.

But then we all have our views on other people's marriages. 'I wouldn't be married to him if he was the last man on earth.' The truth is that no two couples view the contract in quite the same way. What works for one may be death to another. On the other hand there is no doubt that few of us today will order that relationship in the same way as previous generations. My mother-in-law, who claimed that life with my clergyman father-in-law was like trying to halt Niagara (when she complained about the years of neglect at the hands of his vocation, he always said, 'But I had my work'), often quoted Lady Fisher, wife of a previous Archbishop of Canterbury. After she had addressed the girls of Wycombe Abbey School one earnest pupil asked her if she had ever considered divorce. 'Divorce, never', she said, 'but murder, frequently.'

Shifting social structures, gender and employment issues have changed the state of play whether we like it or not. Yet despite an ever-increasing number of 'partnerships', the married state is still extremely popular. Woman and man are still prepared to take the risk of attaching themselves publicly to one other, thereby renouncing any others they might have had. Or at least, that's what Christian marriage is all about – the exchange of one kind of liberty for another. Here is no licence for oppression, for diminishing each other, but for 'the *mutual* society, help and comfort that the one ought to have of the other', says the Book of Common Prayer.

Sadly, it doesn't always work like that. As some of the pieces in this section show only too well, once we catch a glimpse of the secret inner life of the other, once we touch raw nerves, love is precarious. What Scots preacher Peter Marshall called 'the nearest thing to heaven on earth', can become the highway to hell. And yet, God's gifts, though easily spoilt, can be generously restored and renewed. Perhaps the truth is that we fall in and out of love many times in a marriage, but undergirding transitory passion there needs to be basic understanding, friendship and respect.

Today there are an infinite variety of styles of marriage. Some in the church still believe in a hierarchical system, though they may not be able to define exactly what male headship is. But on the whole most couples feel that the days of clearly delineated roles are over. Instead of a hunter, woman now wants the 'new man' she has beheld in her dreams, a gentle, sensitive lover and friend who shares with her the breadwinning and the drudgery and creativity of home-making. She wants equality, dignity, and above all, individual personal identity. But achieving that end can be a slow and exceedingly painful process when it threatens the way men have understood their role for a very long time.

Love and marriage 'go together like a horse and carriage' says the old song. Not any longer. The carriage is now motorized, and may leave behind, as Carol Henderson suggests, 'a stallion in slippers and shuffling off'. Can we find a comfortable harnessing which accelerates, rather than impedes our progress? We marry with very differing needs, exceptions and styles of communication. Acknowledging the fact and admitting our needs could herald an era of affirmation and appreciation – but it may not happen overnight!

What do men really want of their women? Most were loathe to tell me. Perhaps, at heart, they want someone willing to sacrifice her all for them, as they saw their mothers do for their fathers. Who wouldn't? Only now they can't say so without guilt. Nowhere is that more true than in the professions where women were once expected to be subservient to their husband's career.

In Joanna Trollope's best-selling novel The Rector's Wife, *Anna Bouverie no longer knows who she is. In an attempt to find out, she takes a job stacking shelves in a local supermarket. The consequences for her marriage are disastrous.*

I Am Lonely

He had, it seemed to her now, leaning on her gate, rejected her. All those years of defending him, of understanding him, of trying to interpose herself as an insulating layer between him and his disappointment, appeared to have gone for nothing. He had made it plain over the debris of breakfast that not only did he feel betrayed by her – and after all she'd done! – but that he did not really want her near him. She had tried to touch him at the end of the quarrel, but he had shied away from her, folding himself into himself like the spines of a rolled umbrella.

I am lonely, Anna thought. An exploring tendril of ivy was growing along the gate, and she began to rip it up, in little bursts, tearing its dry brown suckers from the wood. I am, in all essential senses, alone, because it would be wrong, or unfair, to burden anyone close to me with my isolation and my frustration. And it is more than that; it is that Mrs Bouverie is taking over from Anna, and, if even Peter does not want Anna any more, then what is to become of her? Is she to become just a competent

Pricewell's worker with a blue overall and a jolly plastic badge? Is that to be Anna? She looked up at the innocent sky. 'Do you want Anna?' God was probably as little inclined to judge such silliness as Peter had been. Why was it that she was made to feel that her claims had no validity, that her existence was only permitted by everyone as long as it remained relative?

Joanna Trollope

Unlike the Bouveries, many couples do survive the overturning of long-held traditional roles, when there is openness, honesty and a willingness to grow. It was only when she joined a babysitting circle that clergy wife Mary Reid discovered 'it wasn't just clergymen whose jobs had priority over family, and it wasn't just clergy wives who had to take over all the domestic responsibilities. It was a general middle-class fact of life.'

Mary Reid is a teacher. Her husband, Gavin, is now Bishop of Maidstone. When she wrote the following piece, thirteen years ago, he had just been appointed Publications Secretary for the Church Pastoral Aid Society, and she had yet to return to work.

Gavin's job seemed to bring him into contact with many interesting sounding people. Unlike his curacy days he came home in the evenings and was obviously happy to be home. I would question him about who he had met and where he had been and would get fairly vague replies. I'd tell him my news: 'I had coffee with Brenda. Cathy lost a tooth today, and Stuart climbed right up to the top of the sycamore tree by the garage.' A vague 'Yes, dear', told me that Gavin was really concentrating on *Sports Report*. I can clearly remember telling him that a giraffe had come into the garden that day, and he still said 'Yes, dear' in that tone of voice reserved for dealing with things he was not really interested in.

I began to feel a niggling dissatisfaction with my lot. Gavin was so free to come and go as he chose. If he wanted to go out all he had to do was open the front door and go. If I wanted to go out I had to sort out a hundred and one domestic arrangements and find a babysitter first. I felt guilty about this, as God had been so very good to me – and here I was grumbling again, just like the children of Israel. How ungrateful and unchristian. This feeling of letting God down began to grow and fester. Surely as a Christian I ought to be happy to care for my family? Because I was freed from the extra work of the parish I had set myself unrealistic goals – the house must be clean, the garden gardened, the children happy, my mother visited, the neighbours entertained, and I had to do it all with a happy Christian smile. It would have been much better if every now and then I'd gone on strike and demanded that Gavin stayed in to help with the chores, instead of constantly bottling up bad vibes. Suddenly I developed claustrophobia, was put on valium, and slept for most of a fortnight. Small, petty irritations when suppressed because they are 'unchristian' can become a mountain of emotional exhaustion of not recognised and dealt with properly.

Mary Reid

Some men miss all the pleasure of marriage and fatherhood because they are driven by career pressure. But can they see it? One Christmas, after I had slaved for months to make it special, I found myself with a husband so burnt out with work that he crawled to the meal table and slept through the whole occasion.

Here is a classic example of differing marital hopes and expectations. Wisconsin-born poet Ella Wheeler Wilcox's Poems of Passion, *published in 1883, were originally rejected by the publisher for being 'immoral'. It was she who wrote, 'Laugh and the world laughs with you, weep and you weep alone.'*

The Holiday

THE WIFE

The house is like a garden,
    The children are the flowers,
The gardener should come methinks
    And walk among the bowers,
Oh! lock the door on worry,
    And shut your cares away,
Not time of year, but love and cheer,
    Will make a holiday.

THE HUSBAND

Impossible! You women do not know
The toil it takes to make a business grow.
I cannot join you until very late,
So, hurry home, nor let the dinner wait.

THE WIFE

The feast will be like Hamlet
  Without a Hamlet part:
The home is but a house, dear,
  Till you supply the heart.

The Xmas gift I long for
  You need not toil to buy;
Oh! give me back the one thing I lack –
  The love-light in your eye.

THE HUSBAND

Of course I love you, and the children too.
Be sensible, my dear, it is for you
I work so hard to make my business pay.
There, now, run home, enjoy your holiday.

THE WIFE (turning)

He does not mean to wound me,
  I know his heart is kind.
Alas! that man can love us.
  And be so blind, so blind.
A little time for pleasure,
  A little time for play;
A word to prove the life of love
  And frighten Care away!
Tho' poor my lot in some small cot
  That were a holiday.

THE HUSBAND (musing)

She has not meant to wound me, nor to vex –
Zounds! but 'tis difficult to please the sex.

I've housed and gowned her like a queen
Yet there she goes, with discontented mien.
I gave her diamonds only yesterday:
Some women are like that, do what you may.

Ella Wheeler Wilcox

And yet, when a woman decides the time has come to establish her own individuality and independence, be it in working outside the home, taking an Open University course or becoming a school governor, her husband may find it very difficult. 'For our generation', says Mary Reid, when she became a working wife, 'this means a husband has to swallow a lot of pride.' She had to swallow a great deal of guilt. 'I don't like Gavin doing the breakfast or the dishes, I feel this comes under the category of "wifely duties". Gavin wants me to eat my breakfast and go off to school, and leave him to sort out the dishes. He sees me off on my bike, and it's a strange sort of role reversal.'

But some husbands are not as adaptable. When Helen North-cott decided, now her children were at school, to go back to college, she had no idea how negatively her husband would react. Ultimately separation became the only solution.

There's Meaning Behind Those Caring Words

He said, 'you are not alone
         you will never be alone
         Don't feel so alone
         I

             am
                 here'

But, He is wrong
For, I am
always
alone,
Alone with my problems and my fears.

HE MEANT:
I will not let you be alone
he doesn't want to be alone
and so that he is not alone,
I must
stay
near.

But he is wrong
to take from me
my right
to be
alone
without the company of HIS fear.

Helen Northcott

Writers like David Thomas, who wrote a book called Not Guilty – In Defense of the Modern Male, *think women have been too hard on men. We expect instant acceptance of a radical change in what was an unspoken contract. 'You be a good wife and mother, take care of the emotional housekeeping, and I'll get a job, play football with the kids and not spend too much time at the pub.' (For the Christian man, read church for pub). Women, says Thomas, have been helped by the women's movement to break away from the need to be needed. But a man is equally afraid of being unwanted – as a partner, father, breadwinner – but no one has helped him. The solution? Not that women should turn the clock back, but that we should boost his confidence by offering a little extra loving reassurance in a time of transition, rather than the usual accusation and blame.*

'A married guy is responsible for everything, no matter what', says a tongue-in-cheek Garrison Keillor in his Book of Guys. *'Women, thanks to their having been oppressed all these years, are blameless, free as birds, and all the dirt they do is the result of premenstrual syndrome or postmenstrual stress or menopause or emotional disempowerment by their fathers or low expectations by their teachers or latent unspoken sexual harassment in the workplace, or some other airy excuse. The guy alone is responsible for every day of marriage that is less than marvellous and meaningful.'*

Self-centredness and insecurity, be they in a husband or a wife, are highly destructive.

Episode of Decay

Being very religious, she devoted most of her time to
    fear.
Under her calm visage, terror held her,
Terror of water, of air, of earth, of thought,
Terror lest she be disturbed in her routine of eating her
    husband.
She fattened on his decay, but she let him decay without
    pain.
And still she would ask, while she consumed him
    particle by particle,
'Do you wish me to take it dear? Will it make you
    happier?'

And down the plump throat he went day after day
  in tidbits;
And he mistook the drain for happiness,
Could hardly live without the daily nibbling . . .
She had eaten away the core of him under the shell,
Eaten his heart and drunk away his breath;
Till on Saturday, the seventeenth of April,
She made her breakfast on the edge of his mind.
He was very quiet all that day, without knowing why.
A last valiant cell of his mind may have been insisting
  that the fault was not hers but his;
But soon he resumed a numbness of content;
The little cell may have been thinking that one dies
  sooner or later
And that one's death may well be useful . . .
For supper, he offered her tea and cake from behind
  his left ear;
And after supper they took together the walk they
  always took together after supper.

Witter Bynner

There are certain dangers in drifting into parallels with the pet world, especially when it involves prayer and healing, but nonetheless, the following little birdie story makes an interesting response to Witter Bynner's man-eater.

Gordon Dalbey is an ordained United Church of Christ minister, leading spiritual growth groups in local churches all over the United States. His book, Healing the Masculine Soul *was a response to the realization that men are in crisis. Since the sixties, he says, when women demanded they lay down their macho-ness and become the 'new man', they have been feeling 'fearfully lost and vulnerable'. Strange, I thought they were*

74

*totally emasculated in the late forties and fifties when an army
of frustrated females, taking revenge for being denied access to
the postwar job market, made them believe they couldn't cope
with picking up a duster, boiling an egg, or making themselves
a cup of tea.*

Noting that he had two birds, a male and a female, in the
cage together, my friend recalled coming home one evening
to find the male leaning lethargically against the side of
the cage, his head hanging low. Concerned, he was about
to open the cage door when the hen darted across the cage
and began pecking furiously at the male, who only shifted
weakly even when she tore tufts of feathers from his
wing. Upon closer inspection, my friend noticed from the
male's outward appearance that the hen must have been
attacking him for some time.

Not knowing what else to do, he took the male from
the cage, and sat down, holding it in his hands. He then
simply began praying for the bird's healing. After perhaps
a half an hour, he decided to put the male in a second cage,
alone and apart from the hen, and to call in the vet in the
morning.

When he had placed the bird on the empty cage perch,
my friend was surprised when, after a moment, it began
to chirp, quietly at first, and then loudly, with great gusto.

'He kept on chirping brightly, until I knew that was no
sick bird any more,' he said. And so he put him back into
the original cage.

Together we marvelled at this amazing story of God's
healing. And then, it occurred to me to ask: 'But what
happened with the hen?'

'Well, that was amazing too,' he declared. 'Not long
after I set the male back on the perch, she came right over

after him, as she'd apparently been doing all day before I came home. He just sat there as she came over, but when she went ahead and took a peck at him, he flew into a raging screech and charged back at her furiously, pecking at her. He didn't follow her over to the corner and hurt her, but as soon as she flew off away from him, he went back to his position and began preening himself. After that, she never pecked at him again and they were chirping together before long.'

Today, when working with the 'hen-pecked' male who is afraid of the woman I tell this story and ask him, 'Where are you personally in this story? Are you sick and weak, allowing the woman to destroy you? Or have you dared to separate yourself from her and place yourself in God's hands for healing – that is, have you responded to the Father God as He calls you out and away from your mother? Or have you allowed God to heal your wounded masculinity and then re-entered the cage and re-engaged the woman with His strength and courage?'

Gordon Dalbey

Why does no one ever talk about a 'rooster-pecked' wife? There are plenty of them around – even if the rooster fails to recognize that he's pecking.

Dr Jim Watts, anaesthetist at the North Staffordshire Hospital, was brought up in a working-class Irish home, the son of a fiercely orange Presbyterian father and Catholic mother, who had mixed feelings about his chosen profession. He couldn't understand at first why his mother was disappointed that he had become an anaesthetist, until he realized she thought he had said he was an atheist.

My father told me when I started at medical school that he only wanted me to discover the reason why it was the men who got all the heart attacks and ulcers, and not the women. After my first year, I explained about stress, lifestyle, fats and oestrogens. He disagreed. 'It's because,' he said, 'men keep their troubles to themselves, but women insist on passing theirs on incessantly to their husbands. Result? The men get double the stress and burn out before their time.'

Mum replied that women carried all the world's troubles, always suffered the birth of children who broke their hearts and lived in a virtual living hell, always second best to their man.

'Ah', replied Dad wisely, 'but there is an up-side. You get to live longer.'

Jim Watts

It is galling for a man that his wife will usually have the last word simply by outliving him.

Carol Henderson is a qualified Myers-Briggs personality typology consultant. A writer and occasional broadcaster, she also shares in husband Stewart's poetry readings and workshops. The conflict between man and woman has been a regular theme in her writing. This piece captures so well the way we can erect brick walls to keep each other out.

War, Outright War

MALE	FEMALE
I want to win this war	I want to win this war

and being war, I have plans	and I have tactics
broad offensive of strength	a sniper's determination
the authority of leadership	a small package strategically placed
Here in the briefing room I move flags around and issue orders	When overruled, the oppressed resort to cunning
i.e. manipulation	i.e. survival
She's over-emotional	He is as communicative as a deaf slug
always shopping shopping shopping	a pack of nappy liners baked beans some Danish Blue and a half of Johnny Walker to help me cope with you
Her ceaseless flow of words. I married a babble from Outer Space.	And how was your day dear? Oh, pretty quiet here in the foxhole with my Safeway trolley – I lost the children, carried out a daring raid on the off-licence and macheted the postman.
That's nice, dear. And so Thompson says to me, 'Let's go for a drink, I've got various proposals to put to you . . .	He's a verbal croupier, dealing only with what is necessary

78

She always exaggerates

He never talks, only repeats

I didn't ask to be a man

He seems to have just two
emotions – silence or rage

This is not anger, this is
called being provoked

Now the lion has pounced
from his cage and soon all
will be blood

She just won't let the
matter drop

invade, colonize, subjugate

Yes, I know all men are
rapists

It was once desire, now it's
habit

It was once so special, we
were both so eager

He's like a pneumatic drill,
it's wonderful when it
stops

Is this how it must be, a
stallion wearing slippers
and shuffling off?

He is in there, somewhere,
shivering in an undis-
covered cave, frostbitten
by the past, full of loud
fears

She seems fuller than me
more able
perhaps God got the labels
wrong

And I with my child-bearing
hips stand astride the two
galloping stallions called
belief and disintegration

Carol Henderson

*'We take our shape from the damage we do each other', says
poet Elaine Feinstein. And yet there are compensations. Even
with the problems, and all the unmet needs, what would life be
without each other?*

*Elaine Feinstein is a prolific writer with several novels and
books of poetry to her credit. Born in Lancashire in 1930 she
was raised in Leicestershire in a Jewish family, and was an avid
writer as a child. She won an open scholarship to read English
at Newnham College, Cambridge. 'A few years later, when I
was married with two children, I began to start writing again.
It was a particularly bleak time of my life. I was altogether
unsuited to housewifely responsibility (though I have always
been grateful that I took the risk of becoming a mother of three
sons), and could not make friends easily with the women who
lived round about me on the housing estate in Cambridge. And
I was as much emotionally cut off from the world round me as
if I had been divided from it by glass.'*

Marriage

Is there ever a new beginning when every
word has its ten years' weight, can there be
what you call conversation between us?
Relentless you are as you push me
to dance and I lurch away from you
weeping, and yet can we bear to lie
silent under the ice together like
fish in a long winter?

We have taken our shape from the
damage we do one another, gently as
bodies moving together at night, we amend
our gestures, softly we hold our places:

in the alien school morning in the
small stones of your eyes I know how
you want to be rid of us, you were
never a family man, your virtue is
lost, even alikeness deceived us
love, our spirits sprawl together
and both at last are distorted

and yet we go toward birthdays and other
marks   not wryly   not thriftily
waiting, for where shall we find it, a
joyous, a various world? in fury
we share, which keep us, without
resignation: tender whenever we touch   what
else we share   this flesh   we
bring together   it hurts to
think of dying as we lie close

Elaine Feinstein

Sometimes it takes a crisis to jolt us into recognizing that the relationship is a gift to treasure, not squander.

Sam Hill has his own computer graphics business in Lancaster. A professional musician, he has played with his band at gigs all over the country, and at many Christian arts festivals, including Greenbelt.

I was the perfect Christian man – until the day Isabel told
me she didn't believe any more. In that terrible moment I
knew I was a sexist, chauvenistic, selfish phoney.

What are phoney Christian men like? They mistake

81

evangelical culture for real religion; they confuse appearance with true character, jargon with spiritual maturity; they seek status, not saintliness; they spout, they don't listen; they're high profile, not holy, committed to meetings, not marriage.

We'd been married four years, Isabel and I, lived with two babies in a council house in a state of virtual penury as I had no work. I thought things couldn't get any worse. But they did. She told me she didn't want my God any more. It felt as if she didn't want me.

What was there about me to want? Like most other men I had treated the woman who meant more to me than life, as an extension of my life, not having her own. 'I'm going to have a pretty wife to run round after me and make my tea.'

In a flash I saw myself as I was, stripped, naked, with nothing left, no identity, or security. The panic attacks were so bad I could hardly get our of bed. I couldn't even write a song. I fell into a deep, dark hole, and no one, certainly no male-dominated evangelical culture, could pull me out. 'Take me and break me.' We say it so easily. It's bloody awful when it happens.

Then at last God himself climbed in and rescued me. It was God alone, just him and me. My brain woke up. For years I'd been, 'up the Clyde in a banana skin', as my wise old Dad used to say. Everything I thought mattered, didn't. Everything I'd neglected, did. From now on it was God, wife, kids, supporting them, in that order – and everything else was a bonus.

Bel went back to college to get the education she had missed. I cooked, cleaned, put the kids to bed. I knew I had gifts God could use, but he said, 'Wait, wait, just wait. I love you and Bel. That's all the matters.'

And now it's all there for me, success in the graphics business, gigs all over the world, the lot. But Bel still claims to be an atheist. And that keeps the priorities sorted when my maleness threatens to bulldoze her over. Self-centred, egotistical, ambitious, men have a raw deal. We need status for credibility. And that's what ails the church. Women don't have the need for status programmed in.

But thanks to Bel I know what and who I am as a man. I've learnt to cry, express my emotions, be a giver rather than a predator in sex. Best of all I'm infatuated with my wife. I fall more in love with her every day. And I can't risk losing her.

Sam Hill

Martyn Green is a 54-year-old Anglican clergyman, married to Anthea. They have two children at university. In 1991 Anthea had breast cancer, 'an event which had a very profound effect on us all. The children, then eighteen and seventeen became adults whilst supporting both of us. I was terrible, not just because of the illness, for that happens to one in ten of the female population in this country, but because my lovely wife was scarred, angry because although the treatment was excellent, we were patronized, angry because I felt helpless, left out. My position as the partner of a breast cancer patient, like so many other partners, was summarized in the immortal words of a GP practice nurse who said to me recently. "Oh, we don't consider the partner at all." Thankfully things are beginning to change – albeit slowly.'

The Helpless Onlooker

The partner is made to wait while the examination
is made –
too risky to see the beloved's body viewed, pummelled
and pressed.
The partner too often is made to wait whilst the news
is broken,
only being summoned to console –
but far too late to shed the same first tears and clutch
the shaking body.
Plans made and remade; decisions taken or deferred –
for 'the choice is yours!'
But can we really weigh the risks – do we truly
understand them?
Is this invasive thing more virile than our fear?
Will someone please admit 'we don't know'.
All too soon there is the scar, a huge
laceration of body followed quickly by internal
violation of mystical rays and heavy metals.
Soreness, sickness and if young even more dramatic
changes.
If only the professionals would share their
lack of knowledge, how much more courage
it would give us – for we feel helpless too!

Martyn Green

*For better, for worse, in sickness or in health, despite the
minefields, the failures, and the blame, we go on committing
ourselves to each other. Why? Is it lunacy or masochism? Or
because, in the end, Peter Marshall is right? Nothing else on
this earth compares with that one special relationship.*

I'm in the Dark with You

I tried to surround you
forgive me, I'm male
I'm a timid lounge lizard
who's just lost his tail
Now I'm in the dark with you.

I do tend to rush things
It's masculine drive
I'm Romeo on
a King's Cross 125
And I'm in the dark with you.

I'm completely unmoved
by a gloss centrefold
I'm thoroughly houseproud
a new man for old
But I'm still in the dark with you.

Nocturnal confusion,
the silence of doubt,
and how to avoid
being laddish throughout
When I'm here in the dark with you.

Maybe it's hormones, maybe it's fate,
it's certainly gender that gets us in this state
but now all I wish is to stay awake late
and be still, in the dark, with you.

Stewart Henderson

7

Fancies, Follies and Fantasies

And do you not know that you are Eve?

The sentence of God on this sex of yours lives in this age: the guilt must of necessity live too. You are the devil's gateway: you are the unsealer of that tree: you are the first deserter of the divine law: you are she who persuaded him whom the devil was not so valiant enough to attack. You destroyed so easily God's image, man. On account of your desert – that is, death – even the Son of God had to die. And yet you think of nothing but covering your gowns in jewellery? You should always go about in mourning and in rags.

Tertullian (160–225 AD)

Women, unlike men, radiate sex, and their temperament is inappropriate in church. . . . Their ordination would introduce distractions and earthiness into worship.

An anonymous bishop in the 1990s.

Will all the women present please cross their legs and close the gates of hell.

Billy Sunday, nineteenth-century evangelist

Women need a reason to have sex, men need a place.

Billy Crystal in City Slickers

In June 1995, actor and film star Hugh Grant, a man with the most beautiful women in the world falling at his feet, was arrested in Hollywood and charged with committing a lewd act with a prostitute. That a man should risk his reputation and career for a moment's pleasure emphasizes the utter incomprehensibility of the male sex drive for most women. But if male sexuality is a mystery for women, how much more is female sexuality for a man. Nowhere are our differences more marked.

Most men I have spoken to fear their libido. 'Am I normal', they ask their mirrors every morning, 'or a distortion of nature?' And of course women are so reassuring: 'You're sex mad. No normal man could possibly want it as often as you.'

The poor souls are buffeted and tossed on the turbulent billows of their rampant male hormones, which carry them helplessly along on the tide, while we women are left behind on the shore with a vague feeling of inadequacy. We do have sexual desire, of course we do, but barely get round to acknowledging its rumblings before being overcome by the torrent of testosterone on the other side of the bed.

'But you never initiate things', says he, peevishly.

'I never get the chance', complains she, through gritted teeth.

'Every male I know wonders whether he's missing out on something', says American psychologist Dr Archibald Hart in *The Sexual Man.* Of 150 'good, clean, average, men', asked whether they felt their wives understood their sexuality, 83% said no. 'This no answer often reflects frustration at not getting enough sex', says Dr Hart. What a surprise! From conversations with female friends, and from the pieces men have written for me, many of them seem to feel solely responsible for keeping up the national weekly average. Others find that an intolerable burden to bear. But they never discuss it with each other. It's too loaded, too enmeshed in the complex web of male achievement, success, and virility, to take the risk of finding out whether you're normal or not. 'Religious men, more than non-religious men', says Dr Hart, 'don't talk about their sexuality, so they never get an opportunity to be honest with themselves and with God. And if there's no self-honesty, there can be no integration of the sexual side of a man with his spiritual side. He splits, developing two sides of himself which are continually at war.'

A Radio One DJ recently said that men think about sex every seven seconds. One of my Christian male friends thought that a very niggardly estimate. 'Men think about work a great deal of the time, food most of the time, and sex all of the time', he said. 'Can I quote you by name in my book?' I asked. 'Certainly not', he said.

There is no area more fraught for the Christian, more beset with the landmines of shame, fear, hypocrisy and confusion. Despite our so-called 'open society', despite an unhealthy obsession with sex, we are more secretive about our sexuality, more repressed than ever. The fact that church ministers sometimes fail to handle their sexuality appropriately, particularly when they confuse it with power, only adds to our general unease. We find it hard to believe that that erogenous zone of ours, the imagination, is as much part of God's holy creation as the bits of our selves we like so much better.

Why did God create such a discrepancy in the sexual drive of men and women? Why is chemistry so much more important for a woman than it is for a man? Why can't a woman have pleasure purely from the reproductive act the way a man can? Why, if sex is a gift, does it come with strings attached, like limitless fertility? Why doesn't our faith deal with all our sexual hang-ups and answer all our questions? So much mystery. Perhaps we'll never know. But one thing is sure, unless we actually explore the issue and hear what the other has to say, there never will be any real point of contact, no chance to explore what makes us so different, and rejoice in it. This is where we make a start.

The Revd A. Studdert Kennedy, known as 'Woodbine Willie', was an army padre during the First World War. His poetry managed to say for the lads on the Western Front all they ever wanted to say for themselves. God may well have been an important feature of life in the trenches, given the horror the men faced, but realistically, certain more earthly fantasies were bound to distract a man from his religious duties.

Temptation

Pray! Have I prayed! When I'm worn with all my
praying!
     When I've bored the blessed angels with my
     battery of prayer!
It's the proper thing to say – but it's only saying, saying,
     And I cannot get to Jesus for the glory of her
     hair.

G. A. Studdert Kennedy (1883–1929)

If fear and confusion lie at the heart of our sexual attitudes, it's bound to come out in the church. Who can forget, in those hard and heady days of the debate on women's ministry, the words of one clergyman who said women couldn't be priests because they wear distracting, dangly earrings? John Stickley in his diary, written in 1991, captures another of those great dilemmas.

The Great Nipple Debate

What is an adult, intelligent, creative man doing sitting on a hard wooden pew on a Sunday morning listening to a sermon warning of the dangers of cuddling women? (Apparently we must guard against sinful desires which, if unchecked, could lead to hugging a person of the opposite sex in a way that says more than 'I hold you in high regard, Sister Christian, and I would like to encourage you'.)

I am a hugger, dear diary. I love hugging and cuddling. I love to hold people in my arms. I kiss ladies' hands. I tell them when they look nice. I kiss men. I cuddle men. I also kiss and cuddle cats, dogs, photographs.

The church has a big problem with sex. (I appreciate that I am not the first person to realize this.) Sex is the difference between men and women. Sex is what makes women and men attractive to me. Men are different to women. I am a man. I love the difference.

It's the fault of the sixties. Sex was invented when I was about ten. Now we read about sex, we talk about sex, we educate about sex. We are not afraid of the freedom to discuss sex, but we are afraid of sex. We are not generally capable as a race, certainly as British, of celebrating the difference between men and women. We need liberation, and the church has the biggest problem of all because it confuses sex with the sex act.

When Marion choreographed a dance some years ago she encountered a problem. The performance was to be in church. The dancers were attractive women – in leotards. The church was faced (if you looked closely) with the sight of six breasts, tightly covered with smooth fabric.

There then followed several intense weeks of 'The Great Nipple Debate'.

Finally, despite pressure to (decently) clothe her dancers, Marion and her young women decided to dance to the glory of God, nipples and all.

If the church wants to be my moral guardian, it will have to learn the difference between what comes naturally and what people may or may not want to do with it. That's the way God made it.

John Stickley

Are men really so helpless that they have to be ruthlessly pro-tected from their inner urges? Fundamentalist Islam has come up with the logical conclusion: purdah. But it isn't actually an effective deterrent. A friend of mine who was a missionary in Morocco, where women were veiled from head to ankle, told me how the men would line up outside the mosque staring at the women's feet. Neither repression nor oppression is the answer.

I have it on good authority – from several of my 'sources' – that a man can be as aroused by a pair of Doc Martens as a décolleté, by a long, floaty skirt, as by a short one. Admiration and flirtation are not the same. Admiration is a joyful part of being human. Flirtation is exaggerated eye contact, excessive attentiveness or empathy, inappropriate flattery. This is the tee-tering on the edge of what the woman priest in the 'Friendship' section called 'the big black hole' at the centre of the other's

*being. The craving for affirmation and adoration, the unwhole-
ness inside each of us, has far more explosive sexual potential
than what we put on the outside.*

*We each need to take responsibility for our own inadequacies.
And that is just as true in the bedroom as anywhere else.*

By far the most common reason that married men gave
for not having their sexual needs met was that their partner was not ready for sex at the same time they were.
. . . For most women these days, life is more stressful and
fatiguing than it is for men. Working full-time, caring for
the house, raising the kids, feeding the family, walking the
dog, pulling the weeds, washing the clothes, and sometimes
even paying the bills – these don't leave a lot of energy for
sex. Add to all these factors poor sexual technique of
many husbands and women are not very interested – for
good reason.

Men who want a better sex life not only need to learn
how to be better lovers, but also how to carry the
emotional and physical burden of home-making and
child-rearing. To put it bluntly: many men only have
themselves to blame for their low sexual satisfaction

Archibald Hart

*Well, that's a beginning, Dr Hart. But will more domestic help
in the kitchen turn us into wanton strumpets in the bedroom?
Women are capable of great sexual passion, but we're also
extremely complex creatures sexually, martyrs to our hormonal
cycles, terrified of unwanted pregnancy, heavily dependent on
mood and atmosphere. But any suggestion that women want*

love, while men only want sex, is erroneous. Ultimately, male or female, we long for intimacy. The problem is that for women intimacy is the way to sex. For men sex is the way to intimacy. And that's a potentially explosive cocktail. For example, when she feels like saying no, he may feel it is a personal rebuffal. This is what one man said to me:

I used to think, 'Why won't she respond? She's gone off me.' And then I wondered if she was just being awkward, using sex as a weapon, I suppose. After all, it never happens to couples on the television. Now, after nearly thirty years, I've learned that when she says no it usually means there's some other problem in the relationship we need to look at. I just wish I hadn't had to learn it the hard way, that someone, my father or anyone, had explained to me when I first got married that basic mystery about women.

Woman's inability to understand the male sex drive often leads her to censure men, rather than offer compassion and support. Hardly surprising if she has been the victim of its misuse, harassed, exploited, degraded by pornography, but with a world of powerful sexual images bombarding the most vulnerable area of the masculine psyche, condemnation and blame is hardly a helpful response.

'You should tell them masturbation is wrong', one female member of the congregation said to my husband after he had preached on sexuality.

'But the Bible is silent on the subject', he said to her. 'For generations young people have agonized over it. I don't want to add to their guilt. It's up to each individual. And besides – as a woman you can't possibly understand the pressure men face.'

'Ah', she went on, 'but it's the fantasies attached to it that are wrong.'

And how, he wondered, does she know what fantasies form in the male mind, what triggers them, when, where and how often? And if she did, could she cope?

Here is a selection of comments from men:

'I love my wife dearly, but that doesn't stop me from window shopping.'

This is a clergyman: 'When I'm wearing my dog collar I have to remember not to turn my head and stare at an attractive woman. I take it off first.'

And this is my husband: 'I had a wonderful dream about you last night.'

'Are you sure it was me?' I asked.

'On second thoughts, she had longer legs than you.'

Do I feel insecure? There's no point. Where is the woman who can control her partner's thoughts and dreams?

That leaves us with a biblical concept, regarded by our society as a dirty word: self-control. The sex drive cannot remain an unchecked force. However difficult, each individual has to learn their boundaries. And it will vary. This is how one man, a married man, came to terms with his particular problem.

I am a happily married vicar with an amazing wife and three smashing children. Apart from a libido sometimes dissipated by overtiredness I have a highly satisfactory sex life. However, only in the last five years have I made progress against a habit that has dogged me for three decades: masturbation.

It's been a long and sometimes depressing journey, but never without hope. All I offer here are my conclusions for me.

I had a happy childhood, though sexual matters were highly taboo. I remember my father's irritation when he discovered I'd missed the optional 'facts-of-life' lessons at school. 'Now I'll have to tell you', he complained. He never did, but it doesn't seem to have made any difference!

Most of my sexual education was of the 'bicycle sheds' variety at the all boys school I went to. As a normal adolescent I began to masturbate, usually on my own, occasionally with my peers. While it was all perfectly normal teenage behaviour, without any pornographic stimulation, it became a habit I could not break.

As a teenager my dormant Christian faith came alive. I had the usual girlfriends. There wasn't much sexual content in those friendships. However, the combination of an evangelical faith with an upbringing which regarded sex as unmentionable had a distressing effect on someone stuck with the habit of masturbation. Those few brief moments of physical pleasure increasingly led to self-recrimination and anguish. Afterwards I was riddled with guilt and sometimes felt I had committed the unforgivable sin.

For the next thirty years this vestige of adolescence clung on to me – or I to it – and spoiled my life. It got to the point where I was afraid to sleep away from home in case I succumbed to temptation.

Some will feel I'm making a lot of fuss about very little. I disagree. For me, masturbation beyond adolescence was nothing to do with sex. It was a turning in on myself, shutting God and others out, inimical to leading an open, available, holy life. It constituted a failure to realize that my body is a temple of the Holy Spirit.

Over the years I have jettisoned some of my evangelical baggage and become more accepting of myself. I've grown to understand that masturbation was part of an unwhole lifestyle, occurring when I was physically, mentally and spiritually exhausted – it was inappropriate self-indulgence. Now I'm trying to lead a balanced life, rather than working all the hours God sends.

From time to time God's Spirit has nudged me to ask for prayer for this. I've taken quite a lot of nudging actually – wouldn't you? – and it's been pretty embarrassing. But when I have asked, God answered, and the habit has progressively weakened. My wife has been understanding throughout.

Most of all there has been the increasing realization that God's love for me is unsinkable and unstoppable. He forgives my sins, never runs out of fresh starts, and is always ready to mend some more of my broken-ness.

There is no one male or female view of sex. No two men or two women ever feel the same about it. But anyone who swallowed the assumption that man's sexuality is straightforward, while only woman's is complex, needs to think again. Here is another honest account of a man wrestling with his sexuality, this time by 'Les', a layman who works full-time for a Church of England diocese.

My Sexuality Is Supposed To Be Straightforward

My sexuality is supposed to be straightforward but I don't experience it like that at all. My ability to make love arises from a complex set of circumstances: my emotional and physical state, what's going on in my life and mind. It's not the case that my partner wearing sexy gear will automatically turn me on, but I feel a failure when it doesn't – and she feels cheated.

I no longer know how to look at women. They seem to want their bodies to be admired, found attractive and be seen to be desirable, but it's wrong to look at them as 'sex objects' or lust after them. What's the difference between lust and desire? Is it so wrong to look admiringly at a good-looking, sexily dressed woman in the street? Is it right if they are in the street and wrong if they appear in a newspaper or magazine?

I feel a member of a rare breed in that I have never made love with anyone other than my wife. I sometimes feel I have missed out on something, but the more I learn about the consequences of affairs, the more grateful I am not to have had one.

I do, however, have a very active fantasy sex life. I oscillate between accepting it as a deep part of me and something to be celebrated, and feeling deeply guilty about it, as though I am in some way letting my partner down. But the reality is that the two seem to go together, so that when I am 'switched on' it is in both directions, rather than the fantasy world replacing sex with her.

I don't actually know what I want out of a relationship sexually. Sometimes I want to make wild, passionate love. Sometimes I want something soft and gentle. Sometimes I just want to hug and be hugged. Sometimes I want to be left alone. I am frightened of the expectation that I will always have an erection at the right time, because it doesn't feel as simple as that. Unfortunately it is rare for my needs and my partner's to coincide. When we have good sex it's very, very good. But that rarely happens. As I get older I am less worried about it. I used to think there was something wrong with me if I wasn't meeting the supposed national average of three times a week. I've given up counting, so I don't know if it's days, weeks or months since we last had good sex. But it doesn't seem to matter.

The basis of our relationship is companionship above all else. We're good friends. That's what I value above all else – being able to talk together, share ideas, observations, experiences. I also value having someone who will tell me when they think I am behaving inappropriately, taking on too much, or withdrawing into myself. Above all, I think, someone to laugh with, who will also laugh at me and help me to laugh at myself, so that I don't take myself too seriously.

But sex can be a source of laughter and fun, can't it? In his book Liberating Sex, *Adrian Thatcher, who is director of the Centre for Christian Theology and Education at the College of St Mark and St John, Plymouth, believes we're too strung up on the verse, 'If a man looks on a woman with lust, he has already committed adultery in his heart.' Jesus, he says, was talking not to a general male audience wrestling with their fantasy world, but to the religious leaders whose hypocrisy he deplored. It's when the thought seed grows into sexual harassment that it becomes an ugly, offensive weed.*

Merriment is an antidote to the deadening seriousness that has attached itself to sexual activity in much of Christian history. Unless sex is playful, it is intolerable. ... It is the patriarchal treatment of sex which makes it a burden, an embarrassment, a constant source of guilt, a male-defined obsession to be overcome by the iron discipline of the will, or best avoided altogether. Merriment is about pleasure, and deep pleasure in our bodies is a precondition of that deep gratitude to God for our sexuality which is itself the key to responsible and passionate loving.

Adrian Thatcher

Little has been written about enjoyable sex in marriage. Perhaps because it isn't always as enjoyable as it might be. Yet the sexual rapport is often a sensitive barometer of the relationship as a whole. At worst it is a threat, trap, weapon, bargaining counter. At best a source of mutual affirmation, pleasure and comfort, a joyful expression of love. John Donne (1573–1631), Dean of St Paul's, with a weakness for adultery, was nonetheless the creator of some of the greatest religious sonnets ever written. This rather steamier piece, however, was written in the days before his ordination.

Elegy to Love

Come, madam, come, all rest my powers defy;
Until I labour, I in labour lie.
The foe ofttimes, having the foe in sight,
Is tired with standing, though he never fight.
Off with that girdle, like heaven's zone glittering,
But a far fairer world encompassing.
Unpin that spangled breast-plate, which you wear,
That th'eyes of busy fools may be stopp'd there.
Unlace yourself, for that harmonious chime
Tells me from you that it is now bed-time.
Off with that happy busk, which I envy,
That still can be, and still can stand so nigh.
Your gown going off such beauteous state reveals,

As when from flowery meads th'hill's shadow steals.
Off with your wiry coronet, and show
The hairy diadems which on you do grow.
Off with your hose and shoes; then softly tread
In this love's hallow'd temple, this soft bed.
    License my roving hands, and let them go
Before, behind, between, above, below.
Oh, my America, my Newfoundland,
My kingdom, safest when with one man mann'd,
My mine of precious stones, my empery;
How am I blest in thus discovering thee!
To enter in these bonds is to be free;
Then, where my hand is set, my seal shall be.

John Donne

It seems that if there is such a thing as a budding new man it might be in the area of his sexuality that the first, tentative signs appear. Most of the men I spoke to who were aware of a major change in their attitude to women, said that they realized that their wives' appetite for and enjoyment of their sexual relationship increased, not decreased with age and maturity. They saw this as their responsibility, a direct consequence of their transformation from predator to lover. And they were pleasantly surprised, it must be said, at how much it improved the quality of sex for them. For any man who doubts woman's ability to give herself to sexual pleasure, this is orgasm from the female perspective.

Orgasm

It is a colour I am looking for
a colour that is all colours
red and purple and bruise blue and gold green
It is a note I am looking for
a note that is all notes
oboe and horn and the small teasing flute

I hunt it down the channel of flesh
but always it flees me

let go, let go and touch this human body
that is mine and is not myself
suddenly it comes to me running, leaping
I offer it to him with a cry like anguish
it bursts, a new planet spinning into life
it burgeons, a dark red rose opening
I am charged electric with atoms humming
I am blown open, am petal, am fragrance, am rose

Veronica Zundel

I asked men to describe orgasm from their perspective and all I got were guffaws, and words like 'fast', or 'explosion'. I wonder whether that's really the case.

All men ask their women the same question. 'What really turns you on?' As if there is some magic key which triggers female arousal. All they have to do is find the elusive thing, and hey presto! A door opens with endless, unbridled passion waiting to be enjoyed all the way to the distant horizon.

Sorry boys, there is no magic key, only trial and error. But perhaps the treasure hunt, with its element of challenge, is all part of the intended fun.

No Sex Please, We're Christians

Society, said the Archbishop of Canterbury, is obsessed with sex. Society may well be, but the church, it seems to me, avoids the subject altogether. It simply doesn't happen, does it? Well not in nice Christian marriages. To judge by many a church teaching programme, we tend to hope that young people will pick up our moral standards by osmosis. We leave them guessing, and what they tend to pick up are some extremely negative vibes. Or as one student at our church said, 'You always seem to be telling us to wait, but never tell us if its worth waiting for.' Fair point. We bang the drum on fornication, but rarely sing in celebration of marital love.

Why are we so coy? Afraid of upsetting the single? They, I often feel, are more in touch with their sexuality than their married friends. They have no choice but to face the issue, and it's hardly a fair acknowledgement of their struggle and pain if we suggest that they're not really missing anything anyway. Is it because sex is such a private matter? Intimacy by nature must be, but I'm not advocating sharing all the gory details, simply having a more open, honest approach to what plays a very large part in our lives.

I saw a film on the television a few months ago called *Two Golden Balls*. Yes it was very near the bone and rather explicit at times, and I'm glad my two children were out, otherwise they would have sent me out of the room. An ardent anti-porn campaigner finds herself in prison with a porn queen, who persuades her that porn isn't evil in itself. The problem is that it has been dominated by men and their needs. But if women take over the market, they will no longer be exploited and porn will be no more that harmless erotica. A dubious argument, but it made me think nonetheless. What is the fine line between porn and erotica, and isn't there a danger that Christians, fearful of crossing the uncertain boundary, reject both, possibly throwing out the baby with the proverbial bathwater? After all, erotica can't be all wrong or why is the Song of Songs, one of the most explicitly sensuous poems ever written, in the Bible?

It is the only book of the Bible to appear in its entirety in the Jewish Prayer Book, and that always puzzled me as a child. Except that Jews have a very earthy approach to sexuality. I still remember my great-grandmother cackling in a corner over some risque story, usually her own. The Torah insists that Jewish men must give their wives pleasure on the Sabbath. Nowhere, girls, does it say that he is entitled to the same. Who said the female orgasm was a 1960s secular discovery? In the entire animal kingdom only human females experience sexual pleasure. It must surely be one of God's special gifts.

The tragedy is that like so much of God's best, it can be abused and spoilt. For as many women who, given half a chance, would love to shout the joys of their sexual union to the heavens, there are those who find it a disappointing damp squib. A certain amount of erotica can help rekindle the flames. I believe God means us to teeter on the verge of spontaneous internal combustion for the man of our dreams, the man he has given us. And there are books and films and music and poetry and art, Christian and secular, to tickle our female fantasies, if we welcome, rather than resist the delicious feelings they inspire. But Christians are taught to mistrust their senses and deny their sensuality. We cover our British prudery with a thin veneer of tight-lipped Christian puritanism and embarrassed couples who are having difficulties in this area deny themselves the extra help they need.

One of my greatest hopes is that my children will grow

up knowing that I am as filled with passion for their father now, as much, if not more than I was on the day we married, enjoying more and more the great gift of our union. And what more could I wish for them in their marriages?

Michele Guinness

8

Some Are Just More Equal than Others

Woman is a violent and uncontrolled animal and it is use-less to let go the reins and then expect her not to kick over the traces. . . . If you allow them to achieve complete equality with men, do you think they will be easier to live with? Not at all. Once they have achieved equality they will be your masters.

Cato

Man is active, full of movement, creative in politics, busi-ness and culture. The male shapes and molds society and the world. Woman, on the other hand, is passive. She stays at home, as is her nature. She is matter waiting to be formed by the active male principle. Of course the active elements are always higher on any scale and more divine. Man consequently plays a major part in reproduction; the woman is merely the passive incubator of his seed.

Aristotle

What men expect mostly from women is service – sexual service, household service, teaching service in the upbringing of their children, or aesthetic services for their social life, and the services of a conscientious secretary. What they hardly look for at all is initiative, ideas, much less advice.

Paul Tournier

I've come to think that I'm rushing to the rescue much too much where Charles is concerned, and that this situation where I devote my whole life to keeping him going isn't healthy for our marriage. We've now reached that stage where I even have to put petrol in his car for him. What does he think that I am, a robot who does all the chores at the touch of a button? I clean his shoes, fill his cigarette case, organise his wardrobe, run his house, control that trout, Peabody, protect him from all the church-women who adore him passionately, make sure he has nourishing meals at the correct times, listen to his moans and groans – and provide sex on demand. Do I ever get any thanks? No, he takes me for granted. It's not right, Charles, it's not right! I know you love me, but you've lost sight of me, lost touch, and now we don't talk any more.

Lyle Ashworth, wife of the Bishop of Starbridge, from Absolute Truths *by Susan Howatch*

Greek and Roman philosophers divided all of life into male and female components, with he on top, and she propping him up from below. To him belonged the doing, to her the being. Of course, had Aristotle been familiar with the Hebrew Scriptures, like the Jews of the time, he would have realized that the Proverbial good wife runs not only the husband, home and children, but also the family business. Perhaps it was their very competence which terrified the politician Cato. Patriarchy was more firmly rooted within Greek and Roman thought, than in the Jewish culture, which educated all women, rich and poor, and became increasingly matriarchal as the years went by. Meanwhile, down through the ages, the church was in no doubt about which tradition it preferred. A very recent industrial tribunal heard the case of a female employee who lost her job in a Christian company for getting married. Wives did not work outside the home, they told her.

We have come a long way since the days when women were officially limited to supportive roles, though some churchmen think we have gone too far in letting them out of the pew into the pulpit. But we women can be the greatest misogynists of all, undervaluing ourselves, constraining ourselves to certain, limited roles, apologizing for our very existence. But then, we do so like having someone to look after. Let a man into your life and before you know it you're cooking his meals, ironing his shirts, waiting on him hand and foot, just like your mother did, in a way you swore you would never do. But then mothering and smothering, belittling and de-skilling soon bring a man down to size.

There's nothing inherently wrong with waiting on some-one. Jesus did it, set us the example, and told us to serve one another. It only becomes a servile task when the role is seen to be inferior, when the server is taken for granted, or when the service is presumed upon or enforced. The missionary or minister's wife may well have been a better preacher than her man, and he may have been better at keeping house. But until the last few years there was little chance of finding out.

Real relationships are about serving each other, acknowl-edging each others' gifts, boosting each others' self-esteem, releasing each other to be the best we can be. But a great mound of ingrained prejudice, traditionalism and fear may have to be moved before we enjoy that God-ordained equality.

Mildly sexist jokes, otherwise called put-downs, have been an effective way of keeping patriarchy alive and well. One preacher I heard said he thought that Jesus needed female followers, 'to cook the food.' Then what did Jesus do on the edge of the Galilee after his resurrection? For many women paternalism from employers, church ministers, leaders and preachers has almost become a way of life.

Lecturer, writer and broadcaster, Elaine Storkey is the Director of the Institute for Contemporary Christianity (Christian Impact), based at St Peter's, Vere Street, London. Her book 'What's Right With Feminism' was the first in Britain to present a biblical foundation for balanced Christian feminism. It was written before the decision in Synod to ordain women in England for the Church of England priesthood.

Women with pastoral, administrative or teaching gifts find in many churches that they must sit back frustrated whilst some man performs very inadequately a task they would do so much better. . . . on the whole most churches see woman as playing only a 'supportive', if any, role in their congregations. Men preach, women listen. Men pray, women say 'amen'. Men form the clergy, the diaconate or the oversight, women abide by their leadership. Men study theology, women sew for the bazaar. Men make decisions, women make the tea . . .

The church then wants women in their 'normal', 'proper' role. It is happiest with women who are supportive and domestic, women who are uncritical and non-threatening, docile, feminine, good followers, hospitable and passive. Most churches are embarrassed with women who feel called to leadership, women who are perceptive and analytical, women who are learned in the Scripture and have developed biblical insights. The best they can do for them is to recognise that if they were men there would be much they can tackle in the church, but as they are women then they simply constitute a problem. Perhaps the answer might be to get them interested in missionary work. There are, after all, plenty of opportunities for women in Christian service and evangelism if they don't mind going overseas.

Elaine Storkey

If she does opt for missionary work, or any other full-time Christian work, she would, until recently, have been well advised to stay single. Being a wife can still force women into what is described euphemistically by many Christian couples as 'joint ministry'. The theory is to share whatever Christian work they do. In practice, for 'joint' don't read 'equal'.

'We must release our husbands to fulfil their ministries', we prospective, little clergy 'wifeys' were advised at theological college by an older, supposedly wiser, now bishop's wife. 'Oh', I said, on my feet before I realized it, 'I thought marriage was about releasing each other to fulfil our respective ministries. I didn't realize I was called to be the parish doormat.'

The Missionary Wife

The missionary wife ought to keep the home clean and in order . . .

She will need to discipline herself to bother him as little as possible with the details of running the household so as to leave him free for his ministry.

She should serve nutritious meals as attractively as possible, always bearing in mind that his health, and that of her family, are to a great degree in her hands.

She should strive to keep his clothes in good repair –

and this is quite a feat for some missionary wardrobes, especially as a term on the field nears its end.

She can plan to relieve him of the greater part of the burden of letter-writing, saving him hours upon hours of time.

She should share actively in many ways in the ministry to which they have given themselves, assisting him in public or in private, but keeping always in the background.

She should protect him, if possible, from interruption in times when he desires to be alone for study or for prayer.

She will ask the Lord to guard her heart from the taint of jealousy, and to teach her rather the ways of trust, helpfulness, and full delight in her dear one. She will recognise his worth, and show it to him in a hundred quiet ways.

She will make every effort to be attractive for him, even out in the jungle or just 'at home'. Neatness and cleanliness and a happy spirit are irresistible companions.

She will cultivate the qualities of sympathy, perception, and courage which will enable her to strengthen him when he is in need, whatever the cause.

Joy Turner Tuggy

And so it continues, a sorry indictment of the way men are supposed to grind to a total standstill when their women were no longer there to cater for their every whim and prop up their flagging egos. Imagine, heaven forbid, how the kingdom of God would survive if his stomach was empty, his underwear dirty, or his bodily needs allowed to go unmet?

What about her needs? Who cares about her health, spiritual well-being and morale? And why, if she recognizes that her education, skills and abilities are being undervalued should it be seen as the 'taint of jealousy'? Doesn't the risk of jealousy lie entirely with her companion, who might fall apart if he ever suspected that her gifts were superior to his?

Lavinia Byrne is a member of the Institute of the Blessed Virgin Mary, and as a nun is deeply committed to expanding the ministry of women within the Roman Catholic Church. She believes that in the past women have been so busy looking after men that history relegates them to second place. For example, Bishop Stephen Neil's A History of Christian Mission, *published in 1964, hardly mentions a single woman missionary, though women made up two thirds of the missionary workforce, and were responsible for some of its greatest achievements.*

The missionary women's story is subject to the same forms of suppression as those of the other women spiritual writers and theologians and mystics. At its best this suppression happens by accident because women's history is somehow deemed to be less important than that of men and so it fails to get told. And women themselves collude with this silence by not taking their experience sufficiently seriously, so not bothering to write it down. Or worse by keeping silent out of a warped desire to avoid vainglory.

At its worst an actual dynamic of suppression is operating. This means that what women were writing or talking about was not liked and so their access to the printed word was inhibited. Their books were printed in small numbers by publishers whose good will alone could not guarantee their survival. They are in limited supply nowadays, curiosities in second-hand bookshops or space fillers in charity and thrift shops. The major great histories of the missions published in this century virtually ignore them. But present-day histories are often just as well guarded. And so there is a reluctance to name the wives of the 'true greats' like David Livingstone – Mary (so frequently abandoned); or William Carey – Dorothy (who died from sheer misery); or Nicolaus von Zinzendorf – Erdmuth (who was deceived by her husband), just in case the truth should backfire and raise ugly questions about the extent to which a man's call to ministry should be exercised at the expense of his call to marriage.

Then there are questions raised by the very nature of the missionary women's ministry. When they took on the agenda of justice and began to question the cultural norms which meant that women's feet were tortured and bound in China, that widows were killed in India, that twin-children were slaughtered in Africa, that girl children were forced into prostitution and grown women into zenana harems, they challenged a world which had been established by men for the convenience and servicing of men, whatever their religious tradition. Islam, Hinduism, the African religions were judged and found wanting; but then so too was Christianity.

This was why the connections which the missionary women began to make made them a dangerous force within Christianity. The very freedom they professed to proclaim, the gospel message itself, turned round and hit them in the face and demanded that they too become accountable to the Lord of history. When they named the outrage they felt as they witnessed the violation of women's human rights, they raised difficult questions about the place of women in any society, including their own. When they called for change, they were demanding change for themselves as well. When they freed women by ensuring that they should have education, they challenged the entire social structure which, traditionally, had restricted it to men. In a most moving way the journey of the missionary women was a journey into freedom. They purported to bring a gospel of salvation; ironically they found themselves receiving one.

Lavinia Byrne

After such a catalogue it seems a little churlish of Baptist minister David Pawson, to see it as a kind of historical glitch, as if God has a problem matching up revelation and reality. Experience, he says, in Leadership is Male *should in no way blind people to biblical truth. The text, or at least his interpretation of it, is what really counts.*

The shortage of men on the mission field, the unavailability of men to do pastoral work in Korea, the dearth of strong men in the English churches – none of these can 'justify' the use of women in leadership. Indeed, it is an insult to women to use them only because men are not available, with the implication of their redundancy if and when men were available! Before circumstances force us into patterns of expediency, we must first be sure of the principles involved – particularly the question whether sex distinction is relative or absolute, a product of culture or creation.

It is not an historical issue. Church history is a mixed bag. While predominantly chauvinist, there are also many examples of feminine leadership, particularly, though not exclusively, in the last century and this. . . . However the evangelical is not persuaded by the precedent of tradition (either way!), any more than the Reformers were. The churches can be wrong: the Bible, rightly interpreted, cannot be.

David Pawson

It must be said, David Pawson stands in august company. Luther and Wesley both struggled to integrate the abilities of women and the apparent teaching of St Paul. In the end their cultural preconditioning won. Luther, committed to the priesthood of all believers and the spiritual equality of the sexes, still thought women inferior, weak, limited to being wife and mother, and saw no inconsistency in these views. Wesley was embarrassed when he saw how effective women were in proclaiming the gospel, and suggested they only spoke for five minutes at a time, interspersing what they said with prayer. Only George Fox, the Quaker, managed to grant women full equality with men, and the result was a long line of exceptional women.

William Booth also had qualms at first. But it would have been a sad day if the founder of the Salvation Army had agreed with David Pawson. William was a strong, willing, powerful, available servant of God. But even he had to admit that when his wife, Catherine preached, more people were converted.

'Who shall dare say unto the Lord, "What doest Thou?" when He pours out His Spirit upon His handmaidens?' she wrote to him. 'Who shall dare thrust women out of the church's operations or presume to put any candle which God has lighted under a bushel?'

'I would not stop a woman preaching on any account', replied her husband. 'Although I should not like it. I am for the world's salvation. I will quarrel with no means that promises help.'

'Supposing', Catherine said, preaching years later, 'I had held back and been disobedient to the heavenly vision, what would God have said to me for the loss of all this fruit?'

It's a question she should have been able to put to Michael Harper, a clergyman who was once at the forefront of charismatic renewal in the Anglican Church, but who left to join the Orthodox Church after Synod's decision to ordain women to the priesthood. In his book Equal And Different *he rather undermines his argument that women should not lead the church by reducing it to canine proportions.*

Dogs have four legs – at least that is what I always thought until the General Synod of the Church of England in November 1992 voted that they have five. I am writing this book to reassure people that nature is right, because God created it. Dogs do have four legs, and I suspect a lot of other people think so.

. . . I will not be surprised if someone sends me a photograph of a dog with five legs (or more likely three). . . . I will simply point out, without fear of contradiction, that such an animal is a genetic freak.

Michael Harper

The dog may well be man's best friend, but of course Michael Harper isn't suggesting that women are anything like dogs. Or is he? Here he quotes a certain little anecdote from Sheldon Vanauken, friend of writer and philosopher, C. S. Lewis. Forgive me if I'm a little confused, wuff, wuff. Or just a little short on dogged devotion!

He joined the feminist movement in the early 1960s. In his book *Under the Mercy* he tells how the first cracks appeared in his feminist apologia: he went for a walk with his dog Nelly up Cedar Mountain. He thought of the *realities of nature* 'where cows are not bulls nor mares stallions'. His dog nuzzled his hand and he thought, 'how feminine – how ladylike' – she was. He saw what he calls, 'the real world'. He goes on, 'I suddenly and treasonably felt, not that feminism was wrong but that it was – silly.'

Michael Harper

It was in the 1970s that the gender debate really began to rage, in reaction to the publication of fairly radical feminist books such as Germaine Greer's The Female Eunuch, *and Betty Friedan's* The Female Mystique. *Friedan identified 'the house-wife's blight', the feeling that many housewives had of being a non-person, imprisoned in their homes. 'I feel as if I don't exist', they said to her. Friedan thought the only solution was for women to break the bars and find meaning for their lives outside the home.*

Though she later modified her views, many evangelical Christians in the USA were incensed by what they saw as an attack on the traditional values of home and motherhood. Instead of listening to what women were saying about their boredom and loneliness, instead of asking what the church could do to help, they simply told them to be satisfied with their lot, underlining it with an uneasy veneer of scriptural justification. Naive new wife that I was, anxious to please my man and my Christian community, I remember devouring books such as The Christian Family *by Larry Christenson,* The Rest-less Woman *by Beverley La Haye, and of course, the never-to-be-forgotten* Total Woman *by Marabel Morgan, where she advocated meeting your husband at the door when he comes in from work, in pink baby doll pyjamas and white boots. Now I suspect that many British men, confronted with such a sight, would be making a doctor's appointment for her before he stopped to put his briefcase down. But even in the more honest eighties and nineties it was hard to shake off the suggestion that if a woman lost her man's love, she only had her own wilful, unsubmissive self to blame.*

'A woman's vulnerability does not stop at the physical level. It includes also vulnerability at the emotional, psychological and spiritual level. Here too she needs a husband's authority and protection', said Christenson. What if she's single? And doesn't the instinctive competitiveness of men make them equally, if not more, vulnerable?

We are blind to the familiar and we are reticent to change anything which gives us power. . . .

So though men may recognise the existence of male power over women they may see this as something which is good and right. Christian men may even see this as having divine sanction. This makes the problem even worse. In order to change their views such men have to swing through the whole spectrum from seeing male power as God-ordained to seeing it as a barrier to God's purpose in the world. For many men such a shift in perspective will change their world view and alter their behaviour more than any other change in their lives.

Yet I believe that such a shift is an essential part of the pilgrimage Christian men must make if they are to emulate Jesus Christ.

Roy McCloughry

Here is nineties man describing his own personal pilgrimage. He calls it, 'Emerging from Misogyny' – just a suggestion, perhaps, of a butterfly easing itself gently out of its cocoon, to discover, surprise, surprise, that the new world isn't nearly as daunting as anticipated.

Michael Mitton was curate of St Andrew's, High Wycombe; vicar of St Chad's, Kidderminster; and is now director of Anglican Renewal Ministries, based in Derby. He and his wife, Julia, have three children, Joanna, Christopher and Lucy.

Emerging from Misogyny

I found the various arguments for and against the ordination of women very confusing. I knew people on both sides who argued with great conviction, and were quite capable of persuading me they were right. The strong emotional content of the debate only added to that confusion. And yet, as I listened, I couldn't help but notice that often their views were not simply the product of carefully reasoned arguments, but were fuelled by deeper intuitions and feelings. This is why the debate was so disturbing – we were being forced to face inner attitudes to sexuality and gender we had hitherto managed to keep carefully tucked away.

It wasn't long before I found that spotlight turned on to my own soul. What I discovered lurking there was an uncomfortable collection of perceptions about men and women inherited uncritically from previous generations. I became aware of misogyny in both my parents and felt it appropriate to repent of all prejudice towards women that dwelt in my conscious and subconscious world, affecting attitudes to my wife and daughters, to women in general, and to my own sexuality.

There was no thunderbolt in my life, no overnight change, but equally, there was no doubt that there was a change of attitude, which particularly expressed itself in my attitude to the ordination of women. I was no longer confused. I know it is dangerous to be so subjective, but instinctively, I was not only comfortable with the idea, but actually longed for the church to take this decision. It was therefore a lived-out healing for me to travel to Sheffield with a friend of mine who is a nun, so that we could take part in the priesting of a friend of ours – one of the first women to be priested in the Church of England.

Since that time I think I have become more sensitive to the hurts inflicted on women by misogynist attitudes. I am more acutely aware of the sin of misogyny in the church, and feel it has been a serious scourge in our history. But it is my conviction that the Holy Spirit is healing us. I am still nervous of the more extreme forms of feminism, but where it would have once made me angry, I now feel a deep sense of sorrow and shame that my church has been so repressive of women, that the only way to protest is to scream loudly. The whole experience has been a lesson about allowing God's searchlight to explore our inner world with all its prejudices, so that we can react from a place of restoration, rather than perpetuating the age-old cycles of dis-ease by our defensive human techniques of avoidance and overreaction.

Michael Mitton

Paul Tournier had a similar story to tell. He is convinced that there can be no wholeness within male-female relationships until men acknowledge the dark secrets which lie hidden in the murky depths.

My daughter-in-law is an artist, and I like her pictures very much. She is a member of the Society of Woman Painters. The Society was organising an exhibition of self-portraits, and a canvas by Monique had been selected. Naturally I congratulated her warmly, and asked her about the opening and closing dates of the exhibition. It was still a long way off, and I thought I should easily find time to go. But when I asked her the dates again, the exhibition had already happened! You can imagine my embarrassment. Here was I, writing a book about taking women seriously.

Monique said, 'If I had been your son exhibiting a picture, I bet you wouldn't have forgotten the date!'

I do not think her remark was an allusion to the blood ties between me and my son. It had much more to do with the discrimination between the sexes.

Here I was, putting all my conscious sincerity into the writing of this book, and all the time in the obscure depths of my mind there lurked an unconscious contempt for women. Naturally I find the diagnosis hard to take.

Have I any justification for being so surprised? The unconscious is like the geologists' fossils: the deposit of the past, both our own personal past and that of the human race. We all undergo social conditioning. It would be arrogant of me to suppose that I alone had escaped its effect! That incident forced me to recognise that I was then in exactly the same state of mind as the Pharisee in Jesus' well-known parable who prayed, 'I thank you God that I am not as other men are.'

Paul Tournier

There are few institutions where it is more difficult to be a woman than in the police force. But even here the wind of change has blown with vigour, tossing all the prejudices up into the air.

Superintendent Ruth Clark, who retired and married in August 1995, was one of the highest ranking policewomen in the country. This short extract from her story, published in Woman Alive *in February 1996, shows how much and how little attitudes have changed. Many of Ruth's colleagues believe that her example paved the way for the appointment of Pauline Clare as the first woman Chief Constable in the country. It seems no coincidence it was to Ruth's force – Lancashire.*

Ruth had a break from the police force in the early 1980s when she studied for a B.Sc. in psychology at Bradford University, researching interview techniques, and non-verbal communication, but returned in 1983 as Chief Inspector for Lancaster. The 1980s were fascinating years for her with the introduction of many new guidelines in the way female and child victims of crime were treated by the judicial process. 'Because the police force was male dominated I knew that rape and child abuse victims were not handled sensitively. I could have acted locally, but what was needed was a major change of national policy.' She helped to set up and furnish the rape trauma centre in Lancaster, and even today, it saddens her that convictions in rape cases are still so hard to get, relying heavily on the woman's reputation.

And then it was back to Fulwood in Preston, where she started her career as a mere constable, many years before, initially as deputy to the Superintendent, and then, when he retired, as Superintendent in her own right, the only senior policewoman in the Lancashire Constabulary. 'But that no longer presented a problem. Women were more accepted. I no longer had to pour the tea.'

But if that was true of the police force, it certainly wasn't of her church, where women are still very much expected to be subordinate. 'How do you reconcile having such power at work, when it's denied you here in church? Is it your humility?' a friend asked her one day. 'I don't ever think of it as power,' Ruth said, 'more as responsibility. As Superintendent I looked after the staff. Imagine the stress they face, the marriage breakdown. You do develop mechanisms for self-preservation, but you can only harden yourself to a certain degree. There is no way a male police officer is allowed to cry. It would be station news. And he can't let anyone know he's not coping in case it affects his promotion prospects. I hope that as a woman, I've been able to give the men permission to be real about how they feel.'

Michele Guinness

Despite major changes in contemporary attitudes to women, we have yet to rise to Betty Friedan's challenge to respond to the pain of the housewife. One of the saddest indictments of our society is its contempt for work in the home. But since, traditionally, that's a woman's job, it must be inferior, mustn't it? It is interesting to see what happens when a man takes over.

In a recent article in Good Housekeeping, *management executive Torin Browne was made redundant and left holding the baby while his wife became the major wage-earner. 'Take one reasonably balanced male, remove him suddenly from the comfort of his stereotypical environment, lunge him completely into an alien world (i.e. stereotypically female), add one six-month-old baby, stir furiously, bring to the boil and leave to*

simmer for a year and a half, and what you have is a recipe for
potential disaster. . . . I can honestly say I have never worked
so hard in my life.'

There were compensations. 'Discovering I was able to calm
my baby with soothing talk and rock her to sleep in my arms,
all her trust sitting on my shoulders, beat having a BMW hands
down.' Nonetheless, he was back out to work and onwards up
the career ladder at the earliest possible moment. Who am I to
criticize? Like Mr Browne I find myself going out to work for
a rest.

The Housewife's Status

It was almost inevitable, wasn't it? After professional
executive breakdown, and church minister breakdown,
there's now mum-at-home breakdown. I can quite understand it. I've forgotten many things already, like a thousand creative ways to fold a nappy, putting away a post-box
toy in three seconds – with all the pieces in the right
holes, getting up six times in the night while functioning
with a certain lucidity, but I've never forgotten the time I
tried to make dinner for six, filling profiteroles with cream
with one hand, mixing a feed with the other, while franti-
cally rocking a bouncing cradle with my right foot in a
vain attempt to pacify a screaming baby, blue with hunger,
boredom and rage. Then in comes himself from work,
and the meal is far from ready, and that look says it all.
'My dear, you're at home. What have you been doing all
day?' She who once catered for a dozen without batting
an eyelid, whose home was a museum-immaculate, who
met him at the door in full war paint has been de-profes-
sionalised, de-skilled, de-personalised by life alone with a
mini-tyrant inside four brick walls.

No, it isn't the loneliness which pushes the housewife to the brink. We all have to cope with loneliness at some point in our lives for all kinds of reasons. Besides, a busy office can be the loneliest place in the world. Nor is it the menial nature of most of the chores. Well may they numb the mind and stifle the senses, but a large number of the population go to soul-destroying labour each day, which gives them little in the way of job satisfaction. And if it were simply the demands of children which drive the young mum batty, every parent would need medical help at some point in their lives. Especially once the little darlings reach their teens and you suddenly find yourself little more than chauffeur, cook, mender, and a walking bottomless bank.

I am convinced that the major stress for the woman who works at home is very similar to the sort experienced, not by the under-pressure executive, but by those who are made redundant. It has to do with a lack of status, which undermines confidence and erodes self-worth. And it is a virtually unknown condition in the Jewish community.

One of my most vivid childhood memories is the sight of my father walking in through the back door. The omnipotent local GP, delivering health and well-being to the neighbourhood, was suddenly divested of his power as he stood on the doorstep. You could see his face change from authority to subservience. Jewish women, like Sarah, Rebecca, Leah and Rachel, are strong, earthy, and rational. In complete reversal of Christian tradition, in Judaism the men are spiritual, while the women have to be practical enough to run the home and children. And there is no doubt which is seen as the more important.

Far be it from me to applaud the subservience of men. My Mama thinks her non-Jewish son-in-law has far too much say in the running of our home if I let him choose the colour of the new carpet or curtains! The point is that

Judaism is matriarchal. The home is the centre of worship. Woman is responsible for creating the right ambience. That involves the smooth running of events, so that festivals, for example, can begin exactly at sundown, so that the whole extended family can relax into worship and celebration. It means choosing the right food, how the table looks, inviting the elderly and the lonely. It means instilling in your children a feel for the Jewish way of life, so that they will grow up to carry on the traditions of their ancestors. Hardly surprising that no Jewish woman ever says, 'I'm just a housewife.'

For this is not being society's invisible woman. Nor is it playing a Christian second fiddle, the 'back up' for her husband's ministry, running the home well so that he has 'street cred' as a church leader, and is free to rush out to his next meeting with a warm heart and a full stomach. This is different jobs, but equal status. This is the key to community, and God knows how much the gain of women's gifts in the job market costs the church just that. This is leadership, for those who do it well have skills enough to run the church, and even the country. This is ministry, for the future of the church, and even the world may well depend upon it.

Michele Guinness

Why do men get to the top of the executive ladder, while women find it virtually impossible to break through the 'glass ceiling'? Deborah Tannen, Professor of Linguistics at Georgetown University in Washington, has made an intensive study of how men and women communicate. She believes our behaviour, be it in the boardroom, on the shop-floor, or even in the church, reflects the playground. 'Research shows that if there is one girl with a group of boys, they tend to ignore or ridicule her. But if there is one boy in a group of girls they tend to treat him as the leader.'

The problem is that we women are often just too self-effacing. We admit our uncertainties – and that's seen as being indecisive. We ask for information – that shows our inferiority. We give attention to detail – that's small talk. Men on the other hand find it hard to admit weakness, never ask for information, give advice without being invited and fire facts like a gun going off. Why? Tannen says, 'For most women the language of conversation is primarily a language of rapport: a way of establishing connections and negotiating relationships. . . . For most men talk is primarily a means to preserve independence and negotiate and maintain status in a hierarchical social order.'

What Tannen calls our 'conflicting conversational styles' keep women under, and the workplace and church are left very much the poorer. The secret is recognizing the differences and appreciating them for what they are.

This piece, which appeared in a student magazine of St John's Theological College in Nottingham, was written, over a bottle of wine, by Gill and Geoff Kimber, once missionaries in Nigeria and now ministers in Arley, Coventry, and by David and Lesley de Pomerai. While Gill has decided to remain a deacon, Lesley is a priest in Ashton-in-Makerfield, and her husband, a scientist, is a non-stipendiary priest. Though only in her early thirties, Lesley discovered some time ago that she had a very rare cancer and was given a short while to live. A 22-hour operation saved her life. That, she says, has worked in her favour. 'A male priest is acceptable for who he is, but a woman priest has to have other qualifications, for example suffering.'

Irregular Declensions

I express reservation
You protest
She throws a tantrum

I am called
You thought ministry was a good idea
She is campaigning for the feminist cause

I have insight
You are perceptive
She's got female intuition

I defend my principles
You keep repeating yourself
She's nagging again

I have a career
You have a job
She's earning pin money

I am deep in thought
You are miles away
She's depressed again

I am filled with the Spirit
You are charismatic
She is over-emotional

I consider the pros and cons
You worry
She's neurotic

I speak my mind
You get angry
She is aggressive

I like to balance antitheses
You are moderate
She is indecisive

I anticipate
You take risks
. . . .women drivers!

David and Lesley de Pomerai, Geoff and Gill Kimber

Lesley de Pomerai says she once asked God to explain to her why he had decided to be incarnated as a man. 'Because women have suffered enough', was the reply. Roy McCloughry, on the other hand, suggests that because Jesus was a man, he had more power to lay down. The cross therefore becomes a much more radical symbol. For every man and woman the only route to true equality is by a kind of dying.

Between 1989 and 1992 a group of men and women of different denominations, uncomfortable with the rigid certainties expressed by both sides in the women's ministry debate, met in Oxford to discuss the complementariness of men and women in the work God had called them to do. The result of their discussions led to a report which they called, A Fearful Symmetry, *a useful insight into the way the basic lack of understanding between the sexes often blinds us to the riches we have to offer each other.*

Some of the women in our group noted that women seem to have a far lower view of themselves and their abilities than do men. . . . they are often reluctant to express themselves, particularly verbally, and need a great deal of encouragement and affirmation. In discussion groups it is generally the men who speak and the women who listen. It has also been observed that women speak at less length and are interrupted more because they use more hesitant speech patterns, which allow for doubt and the desire for dialogue, but which also seem to betray a self-doubt which proves unconvincing to the methods of such male discourse. Others of us who had been spiritual counsellors to women had noticed this same lack of self-confidence. However, it was remarked that women are much more likely to laugh at themselves (and at men) and to puncture pomposity.

The deepest theological issue at stake here is that of *kenosis*, self-emptying, dying to self, which is central to our christology. For men, that doctrine often involves a wrestle with power and its expression in dialogue. For women, it often involves a struggle with the courage to *be*, and with wanting to apologise in dialogue for their mere existence.

This liturgy, written for the Indian Women Theologian's Conference at Bangalore, India, in November 1994 is an attempt to verbalize an attitude of repentance for the years of pain and loss which inequality has meant. It provides an opportunity to let go of past hurts, so that we can walk together into the future, free of prejudice and bigotry.

A Liturgy of Reconciliation for Women and Men

Leader: We know ourselves to be a people who distort sexuality.

All: We are separated from ourselves, each other and the God of life.

Leader: Let us confess our brokenness.

Women: As women caught in our tradition, we confess that we have helped perpetuate the myth of feminine inferiority by adopting the role of natural followers.

Men: As men caught in our tradition, we confess that we have helped perpetuate the myth of masculine superiority by assuming the role of natural leaders.

Women: As women, we confess that we have been willing to limit our image to that of wives, mothers, and sexual objects for men.

Men: As men, we confess that we have often seen women as sexual objects. We have been a part of restricting their roles to those of wives and mothers.

Women: We confess that we have nor sought our own real identity in Scripture and history. We have failed to trust ourselves and other women. We have been our own worst enemies.

Men: We confess that we have perpetuated religious teachings which reinforce illusions of male supremacy. While we exalt servanthood, we leave the menial tasks to the women.

Women: We confess that we have participated in a system which inhibits and denies self-affirmation and creativity to all sorts and conditions of persons.

Men: We confess that we have paid lip service to universal equality, yet our lives are based on sexual discrimination, and, in fact, we have placed women in subordinate positions.

All: Moved by the power of the Holy Spirit, we accuse ourselves because we have not allowed God to form us as a new people. We confess our sin to God, to the Church and to the World. We pledge to work for reconciliation with one another.

Leader: In the name of our creator, our redeemer, our comforter, you are forgiven. You are freed from the past and its oppression. You are free to move to a new future of mutuality and love, taking into account the sins of the past and not bound by them. The Gift is complete; live in the grace of God's love.

9

The Battle of The Sexes

A necessary object, a woman, who is needed to preserve the species or to provide food and drink.

St Thomas Aquinas (1225–74)

If the standard male role model for Christian women is Jesus, they're bound to be disappointed.

Julian Lailey, comprehensive school headteacher

I never say, 'Men are . . . ', because no two are the same. They're all equally unfathomable.

Marjorie Bevan, twice married.

'Women are irrational.' Fifteen love.
'Men . . . ' Fifteen all.
'She must be suffering from PMT.' Thirty fifteen.
'They're such bastards.' Thirty all.
'Or else she's going through the change.' Forty thirty.
'They're so pathetic.' Forty all.

The war is on. But it never seems like a clean fight. Brute force versus guerilla-style tactics. Their physical and social advantages haven't made men wise. Women have discovered ways and means of gaining the upper hand. Where there is no trust, there can be no truce.

For centuries men have seen women as irrational, indecisive, over-emotional, nagging, gossiping, weaker, made to meet their needs, if not their whims. And women? For them men can be bullies, silent, stupid, weak, vain, sex-mad, or, as Marion Pitman says, just plain boring. Putty in a woman's hands, suggests teacher Sue Hunt, who was taught the art of manipulating and patronizing a man at her mother's knee.

In a recent article in the *Guardian*, writing about the extraordinary reversal that more men than women were calling the Samaritans to discuss their feelings, journalist Ros Coward raised the spectre of what she calls 'Womanism'. 'It seems men can't even commit suicide now without provoking women's contempt. Too weak to survive hardships women are used to, too inadequate to have built up their own support network, people who deserve pity become evidence of the injustice of the inferior sex having power. This is not feminism; it is womanism. Womanism assumes that women are naturally morally superior.'

Born of frustration and bitterness, it may well be, but isn't womanism simply the age-old weapon of disdain? In the last section Paul Tournier admitted the ingrained contempt men have for women. There's a danger in attacking men with their own weapons. It proves the point that women are not as morally superior as they claim.

The difficulty is that men and women contend with such differing social expectations. In a discussion group on gender issues I attended, one woman described how she set up an exercise at a theological college. Single sex groups of men and women were asked to reflect on their childhood. The women loved it. The men found it exceedingly difficult – and were irritated that the women found it easy. 'You only shared personal experiences', they said, 'You didn't deal with the real issue.'

As we discussed this together the men in the group explained why childhood was such a frightening subject for a man. 'It touches on all those threatening areas: his relationship with his father, mother, his sexuality. That arouses all kinds of feelings and feelings are worrying. They lead you into unsafe areas where you may be exposed to being bullied, belittled, diminished. Since men always measure themselves against each other, physically, intellectually, even genitally, they're haunted by the fear of ridicule, of being found out, of demonstrating that they are not the man they pretend to be.'

Men may be physically stronger than women, but I now wonder whether women aren't stronger emotionally. Less competitive, they are therefore less vulnerable. That means men and women have the potential to inflict immense damage on each other, unless we find the strength to lay down the weapons and open up negotiations for peace. And the source of that strength? Acknowledging perhaps that the real battle isn't between men and women at all, but between God and basic human selfishness in both the sexes. Gordon Dalbey says, 'We fear not the woman's power, but our own. . . . A man therefore becomes most concerned about dominating or controlling the woman when he has refused to let Jesus dominate him.'

HOW HE SEES HER

The beauty of a woman is only skin-deep. If men could see what is beneath the flesh and penetrate below the surface with eyes like the Beotian lynx, they would be nauseated just to look at woman, for all this feminine charm is nothing but phlegm, blood, humours and gall.

Odo of Cluny, French monk, Abbot of Cluny 910–17

Nonetheless, the message women receive is that physical attractiveness matters to a man. How does that make a woman who describes herself as 'plain, neurotic and over-intelligent as a teenager' feel? Poet Marion Pitman also says, 'Just never seemed to be what men wanted to be seen with. A strong-minded woman not wanting to be leant on is bound to stay single, unless she's very lucky. Maybe if a nice man had proposed when I was in my twenties – but too late now, too bloody-minded. Never prepared to give anyone dominion over me. That's God's job. And anyway, ultimately, most men bore me – not very patient, you see.'

Autobiographical Fragment

Bitches in heat are kept indoors;
I run in the gutter
I have no pedigree

I live on the edge of the town;
My face is badly painted if at all,
My clothes fail to suggest the curve of breasts,
My hair is untidy.

I do not stand on the street
With the women who trade for cash,
Nor do I sit with the women who trade for
    respectability,

Bargaining harder to own a man;
But I am a woman, who tells the truth –

When I say no I mean no,
When I mean yes I say yes;
Whore, virgin, mother, wife,
Look at me askance.

When I went behind the light
Into the country where time passes slowly
No one came after me,
No one sent out hounds and horsemen
to fetch me back;
I lay both queen and prisoner
Till the arrows of God set me free;
They burned me beyond healing –
You may see the scars on my soul –
And my tongue is a flame –
I am a woman who tells the truth;
And so I can neither bargain my wares
Nor court any righteous man.

Is any man strong enough to admit weakness?
Strong enough not to be afraid
Of a woman who tells the truth?

Marion Pitman

Why is he more susceptible to titillation than to truth? What is he hiding from? Veronica Zundel has one suggestion.

Exposure

look he said
what a big one I've got
flashing his rationality at her
from the dirty raincoat of his philosophy

she ignored him, kept a secret smile
knowing he was only terrified
she might have something better.

Veronica Zundel

So there it is, the real problem lurking at the heart of all male-female relationships, popping up in a thousand different disguises: the male fear of the female. Few men acknowledge it, except in a whisper, yet it's a common phenomenon throughout the entire animal kingdom.

'Mysterious', 'unfathomable', 'threatening', said the men I interviewed, with a touch of awe in their voices. Women were complex creatures, had babies, were powerful mothers.

Huw Spanner, editor of Third Way, *said he found women who were both sexy and clever intimidating, 'I imagine most men would think so to some extent and at some level. Men tend to want to be in control over themselves and their circumstances, and I suspect that many of us feel threatened by the ability of a sexy woman to elicit responses we can't easily control. So we rely on what intellectual advantages we have to reassert our ascendancy.*

'A sexy woman who is cleverer and wittier than you is

seriously intimidating. My nightmare would be to stuck in a lift with Pamela Stephenson and Josie Lawrence. Some men might enjoy it. I think I'd want to die.'

Men are more proud than women and have greater difficulty in admitting their being afraid. This is one of the differences between men and women: women often display their fears openly while men hide theirs. A man will hide them, for example, by means of his authoritarian manner. By one word, harsh and cutting, he stops his wife's talking and puts an end to the conversation he fears. Or else he gives grandiose intellectual and scientific explanations which save him from any personal commitment. He wants to have the last word always, and veils through his over-talking his fear of being contradicted. Perhaps the same end is achieved through a display of anger or, again, through obstinate silence.

Paul Tournier

Men seem to feel safer when in charge. They can't be belittled. That's why they slip so easily into 'pedant mode'. 'I really do know what's best for you, dear. Let me show you.' The nearest my man and I ever come to divorce is when he's teaching me to use the computer or telling me how to drive the car.

According to a lighthearted survey in the Daily Express *of what men fear, there's no limit. Journalist and editor of the* Church Times, *Paul Handley, described its result in the magazine* Woman Alive.

Depression was what I felt after reading through the list. There were the usual worries about sexual inadequacy.

Then there was just ordinary inadequacy: 'A woman colleague being promoted above him.' 'A woman beating him at snooker.' 'When a woman can drink him under the table.'

And, if we needed confirmation of men's general slobbishness: 'Having to hang up his clothes in the wardrobe.' 'Ironing five shirts for the working week.' 'Getting a beer belly before he's thirty.'

Suddenly, there in the middle of these domestic anxieties, was this: 'Having to go to church on Sunday mornings.'

Well, honestly. Are these men or mice? Do they need it spelt out? If they were a little less fearful of that, perhaps they wouldn't have quite so many examples of bad behaviour to fret about.

Paul Handley

Why, after a really good row with their loved one, are men left feeling, as one male friend described it, 'like a bag of manure', convinced she doesn't want him any more, and the relationship must be over, while women simply feel relieved that the air has been cleared? Scratch a man and what you'll probably find just underneath the skin, in the most vulnerable places, a terrible insecurity.

The fear of one another as men and women is the greatest block to the mutuality we long for. For myself, that fear first leapt out at me in my high school freshman PE class on rainy days, when outdoor sports gave way to folk dancing in the gym with the girls. In those awkward days of my budding sexuality, I was the youngest in my class and the shortest.

Even today, every time I hear 'Turkey in the Straw' I freeze inside, recalling the awful tension as we fifty-odd boys lined up by height against one wall of the gym while the girls did likewise opposite us. To my utter fear and embarrassment, the last girl in the line opposite me, short though she was, had nonetheless blossomed into precocious abundance. Of course, all the other boys made a great show of wishing they were the shortest, like me, but I now believe they were all secretly glad they did not have to match up against such a young woman themselves.

Because I believe that most of us know that fear from the onset of sexual desire in puberty, I would ask a simple question: what were we – the youngest of men and women – afraid of there in that gym? We all know the answer because we do not lose that fear with age; we simply become more adept at covering it up.

For myself the answer is simple: I didn't want to be rejected.

Gordon Dalbey

Acceptance is what we all want. Rejection is what men feel they often get. As a political reporter for the BBC, shouting questions at slippery cabinet ministers, one might imagine Jeremy Vine the least likely of men to accuse a woman of overriding his emotions – but men feel put down and misunderstood a great deal more often than women care to admit. He has two published novels, Forget Heaven, Just Kiss Me, *and* The Whole World in My Hands – *both about the church, faith and love. He goes to church, has a faith and is in love, he says.*

This poem is 'an attempt to map out concisely the space between two people, an attempt underpinned by a very personal sense of frustration. The writer feels robbed of the only means he has of declaring accurately what is in his heart – and you suspect that if the object of the poem ever manages to read it, she will not even realize she is loved.'

You Say You Do Not Understand Poetry

You say you do not understand poetry,
So I may now write anything I like –
Weave barbs in the text, talk love,
Make gibberish of everything, hijack
Famous works, applaud the Third Reich,
Or pen clichés about the stars above;

Provided they are buried in convoluted
Verse, you will slide those fetching
Spectacles halfway down your nose
And take a razor to the words – hack
Up the pages and use them as confetti.
You want it all in clearest prose,

Laid out like a tax return, totalled
At the bottom, every line correct;
That saddens me. There's not a word
Worth saying can be said like that,
And even dream homes have been wrecked
By surveyors' tools, or the absurd

Dead lingo of estate agents. Fools say
Feelings can be measured like a floor,
Ground up as clauses in sun-sapped

Legal briefs, skewered on a tiny tack –
I say poetry can offer so much more.
Only giant lies are a matter of fact.

Jeremy Vine

Here is another man who feels misunderstood, or rather that we constantly misunderstand each other. Cole Moreton is news editor of the Church Times *and writes for the* Independent *and the* Independent on Sunday. *He occasionally stands on stages at events such as Greenbelt to perform in his own inimitable way. He and his wife Rachel have been married for five years and the border of Essex and London runs through their back garden.*

These are two of four poems, 'if they can be called that', he says, 'based on the things partners say to each other (or rather, don't). Certain kinds of magazines are always carrying articles that say men are supposed to be strong, silent and practical, find it hard to show their feelings, while women are talkative, poetic and emotional. But for a lot of people, the truth seems to be the other way round.'

Dialogue 1

I said:	'It occurs to me, I haven't told you lately that I love you.'
She said:	'You didn't forget to get the milk?'
I said:	'Your eyes sparkle like sunlight on placid summer lakes.'
She said:	'Did you forget to get the milk?'
I said:	'You are a refuge, a harbour for my soul.'
She said:	'You did forget to get the milk.'

Dialogue 2

OK then, I'm here.
Now what? Did you have something to say?
If so, why don't you just say it?

Well, it's just that . . . well . . . I can't say.
It's . . . oh, I don't know.
You can be so damn difficult.

What are you trying to say?
Have you had your fill of me?
Have you? Are you finishing?

No. No. No. Not that. I don't mean . . . no.
It's just that . . . I don't know.
Oh, you can be so damn difficult.

Cole Moreton

HOW SHE SEES HIM

Throughout history women have been seen as the talkers. Research shows the opposite to be the case, especially in public gatherings. Listen in on a church meeting and work out where most of the hot air comes from. Yet though men hold centre stage, real life may be taking place out in the wings.

Knowledge

When the man talks
the woman listens, nods, smiles,
follows a winding thread

146

When the woman talks
the man cuts out, wanders off
goes out of touch

In the man's world
the woman is onlooker, attendant, audience,
congregation

In the woman's world
the man takes
no interest

That is why the woman
knows more than the man
That is why the woman
knows more.

Veronica Zundel

*What many women really want is a man who will chit-chat.
That for them is intimacy: the kind of heart-sharing they experience with female friends. But it isn't necessarily a man's style.
When he resorts to silence it usually means one of two things:
either he feels at home, or he is building a garrison around his
soul.*

He Is a Mysterious Island

The discovery of the real person is never easy. I remember
a woman who had come to speak to me of her very serious
worries. At the end of our interview I asked her, 'What
does your husband think of all that?'

'Oh,' she blurted out, 'my husband is a mysterious island. I am forever circling round it but never finding a beach where I may land.'

I understood her, for it is true. There are men who are like mysterious islands. They protect themselves against any approach. They no longer express themselves, nor do they take a stand on anything. When their wife consults them on something important, they hide themselves behind their paper. They look deeply absorbed. They answer without even looking up, in a tone impersonal, anonymous, and vague, which excludes all argument. Or else they make a joke of it.

Paul Tournier

One area of communication where women feel particularly let down by men is in health care. They complain that male doctors don't listen to them. Women doctors are not always great listeners either, though recent research suggests they do tend to give their patients more time and a greater sense of support.

'We have ways and means of stopping women's periods', a male gynaecologist said to me recently. 'They took everything away and only left me with the bed I was lying on', says a bewildered Thora Hird in a sketch on Channel 4 looking at women's health issues. If male doctors had their way would women be divested of all their spare, reproductive parts? Can a male doctor really appreciate the deeper, psychological implications of what he calls 'women's problems'?

Visiting the Specialist

Across an acre of desk
he sits on his pedestal chair
He is your friend.

He will understand you.
He knows so many people like you.

You must tell him everything.

You must tell him
no more than he wants to hear.

He has glass eyes for looking through.
You cannot tell what they see.

You tell him everything.
He listens to a voice in his head.

He writes you down in his book.
He puts it away. He is kindly,
benign. He has heard no more
than he wanted to hear.

Evangeline Paterson

But how can a man fulfil a woman's requirements when she gives out very conflicting messages about what she actually wants? It's all very confusing for them.

This is 'Les', a lay employee of the Church of England, who described his struggle with his sexuality in an earlier section. He told me that the pressures to be a 'new man' were still so new that he hadn't yet managed to work out the implications.

Being a Man Brings Impossible Expectations

On the one hand to show my emotions, be gentle, vulnerable, soft, enabling; on the other, to be strong, reliable, a shoulder to cry on.

I long to be more in touch with my emotions, and feel a sense of release on the rare occasions when I manage to cry. But it doesn't seem to come naturally.

At times my partner seems to want to manage on her own, to be strong, independent, and woe betide me if I try to 'father' her. At other times she seems to need me with a deep intensity which feels overwhelming, more than I can handle.

If I open doors for a woman, I belong to an appropriate patriarchal world; if I don't, I'm a typical aggressive male barging ahead.

I feel perpetually guilty, not playing a full part in the running of the house and sharing equally in childcare, cleaning, washing, ironing; yet everything in my psyche, and in society seems to drive me out to work, to earn the money, pay the mortgage, be successful.

I know when I do things in the house I'm merely doing a tiny part of my share. But still feel deep down that I'm 'Helping' and should be appreciated for what I do.

I think I have learnt not to take my partner's work for granted. I'm afraid of being smothered by women, taken over by them, suffocated by their breasts – perhaps a hangover from infancy?

I feel I need to keep a distance, keep my boundaries intact. But I sense that isn't what is wanted.

For women, man may be giant – or a permanent little boy,
especially when he gets the toys like a train set out and won't
let the children near them.

When he's ill the world stops. He takes to his bed, or sits
shivering by the fire, absorbing limitless amounts of sympathy.
But when woman is ill his sympathy seems to last as long as it
takes him to go into the kitchen. Whatever he may say about
coping manfully, he has ways and means of letting you know
how lost and helpless he feels. We give in, get up and soldier on,
mother and martyr to the last. It's all a bit of a game really. But
single teacher, Sue Hunt, asks if cheating is the only way to win.

Raised in Ackworth in Lancashire where the soil is hard and
unyielding, the men are tough, the women compliant and
things are not what they seem, Sue had to meet with a man
called Jesus Christ before she could begin to discover a more
honest way of relating to the opposite sex.

Lessons from Childhood

We learned it
When we were very small –
   My sisters and I

My mum
a very thorough teacher.

How to deceive my dad.

Not in the big things you understand –
– just in the small areas,
– the cost of a pair of shoes
– the secretly and carefully planned outing,
   appearing spontaneous to Dad.

No words were ever used in this teaching method
except the ritual chant
repeated often
   'Don't tell your dad,
   He doesn't need to know'

My mum learned it from it from her mum
   who learned it from her mum
     Because
     (we were told)
although men were malleable, pathetic and weak
   they needed us to
     Pretend that we bowed to their opinions
     deferred to their decisions
     abided by their ordinances

while we knew all the time
(we hugged the information to ourselves)
that we, the Women, were
   The Master Race
   The Sisterhood
   The Ones who controlled
   everyone's destiny.

My mother now, she's still a High Priestess
   who excels at her art

While I, am trying to learn for the first time
   how to treat men as equals
   to regard them with respect
   to realize that manipulation
   is no substitute for dialogue.

Sue Hunt

Say What You Mean and Mean What You Say

For a wonderful example of how dialogue between men and women fails, take this little misunderstanding with Jim.

'When are you coming back?' he asked, as he gave me a lift to the station, 'Shall I pick you up?'

'That would be great, thanks', I said, 'Three o'clock on Saturday afternoon.'

'Ah, ah well . . . ' he said, uncertainly.

He was busy on Saturday, I could tell. I didn't want to be any trouble.

'Don't worry, I'll get a taxi', I said, then, as an aftermath, 'Tell you what, if you're not there when I arrive, I'll get a taxi.'

At three on Saturday afternoon there I was standing outside the station in the rain with a racking chest infection. No Jim. No taxi either. I waited twenty minutes, tired, wet and frazzled, until one finally came.

On the way home we happened to stop in traffic outside the church café. Through the windows I saw him, this trusted friend, sitting at one of the tables with a couple of women and a cup of something hot. The toad! 'Right, that's the last time . . . I said to myself, making a mental account of all the favours I had done him, which would cease forthwith. Cut to the heart, I decided to join the mighty battalions of hurt, retreating Christians.

Jews, however, like a kettle on the boil, find it difficult to suppress their hot air. All my best intentions of never speaking to him again dissolved the moment we were face to face, and I said, with Christian love and grace, 'Stand me up would you? Too busy to come for me on Saturday?'

'No. I was bored out of my mind. There was nothing I

would have liked better than to come for you. But you told me not to. You said you'd take a taxi.'

'I said if you weren't there because you were busy, I'd take a taxi.'

'Then why didn't you say what you meant, because I thought you didn't want me to come for you.'

Words, words – but no communication. How many relationships break down on that basis? I can't count the number of times I have driven with my husband down the motorway for miles, desperate to top up, or let out my liquid content, because he fails to respond to my obvious hints.

'Would you like to stop for a cup of tea, love?'

'No thanks, I'm fine', and on we go, I with parched throat, crossed legs, and tight lips.

'I wanted to stop', I eventually shout in sheer exasperation, as yet another service station disappears behind us.

'Then why didn't you say?'

'Because you never ask me what I want.'

You see, I'm thoughtful, sensitive, aware of others, don't put them out, cause them any trouble. I'm a woman. And my husband and Jim, are they insensitive, uncaring, unchristian? No, they're men. We may wish they'd listen more carefully, pick up our vibes, read our small print, but unless they become telepathic, it seems we shall simply have to learn to say what we really mean and want.

When Sarah told Abraham to sleep with Hagar so that he could have a child, then throws Hagar out when she does, Abraham is utterly befuddled. Hadn't he done what Sarah wanted? What if he'd stopped to consider her 'hidden agenda', what if she had been more honest about her feelings of failure and desperation? They may have encouraged each other to wait for God's promise. And how different the history of the Middle East would have been.

And wouldn't our churches be very different too, if women, instead of resenting the way we are passed over and taken for granted, begin to admit our real needs and wishes?

Michele Guinness

'Our fear of one another', says Gordon Dalbey, 'our fear of being vulnerable and rejected was met by Jesus Christ on the cross. If anybody had the right to pull out of a relationship it was the betrayed Jesus; if anybody had the right to call down legions of angels in revenge it was the rejected, abandoned Jesus. Yet Jesus walked the path to the cross, which terrifies our self-centred human nature. He opened the door by which we may risk such vulnerability in our loving relationships today – trusting not that the other partner will change, but that God will not change His saving power for those He loves in Christ.'

This poem encapsulates the power of God to overcome our breakdown of communication. Disabled from birth seven times over, Hilary McDowell is nonetheless a dramatist, journalist, performance poet, counsellor, and deaconess in the Presbyterian Church. She exercises a ministry of outreach and reconciliation through drama, art and music in her native Belfast.

Springing the Word Trap

When talking was,
The man sat dumb.
Freeze dried in tongue and touch
Fled scared enough to fail.
Manacled by memory
Of former Holy Grails.

When talking was,
She wore words like
Spangled truth on neck and arm.
Jewelled messages in sound,
Not knowing that he feared
Cutting edge of diamond.

When talking was,
And hearing ceased,
Annexed communication.
Prayers to spring the word trap,
Prayers to God of union,
Prayed from the Paraclete.

When talking ceased
God sent the Word
Cling-wrapped in straw and stable.
Trussed tight enough to die,
Muzzled by the muteness
Of baby's cry.

When talking ceased
He hung the word
Blood-etched on tree and tomb stone.
Trust strong enough to give
Utterance to the injury
Of those afraid to live

Hilary McDowell

10

Oh What Needless Pain We Bear

Once two Christians fall in love, they never fall out of it again, but live happily ever after in soft focused harmony and unalloyed bliss. We don't fail each other, fancy anyone else, or fall in love with our best friend's spouse. We never lie, cheat or deceive each other. Or do we? If the following pieces are anything to go by, words like pain, hurt and betrayal cannot be eradicated from the vocabulary of Christian relationships.

They may well be suppressed. It's hard to be vulnerable, to take the plunge and admit we have anything less than the ideal, picture-book, Christian marriage. And then church on Sunday hardly provides a conducive atmosphere to admit to the burning resentments, flaming arguments, adulterous fantasies, or spot or two of domestic violence. But they are there, simmering away gently beneath our serene and holy façades.

It may even be the church itself which is the mistress or lover, the all-consuming, adulterous passion which leaves no room for any other. It may be golf or football, a career or a business, all of which are inside our control, unlike the man or woman with whom we're supposed to share our lives, and whose demands are incomprehensible or intolerable.

Can we ever live up to the standards of self-giving that real love requires? The problem is that from childhood on we store all kinds of emotional baggage in the attic of our minds, and we bring it out and hit each other over the head with it whenever we feel insecure, threatened or hurt. Or simply for revenge. At its most basic, says Melvin Matthews, it makes a man trifle with the gift of love God has given him. At its most extreme it can turn into physical aggression. But what is being 'A New Man' – or a new woman, for that matter – if it isn't finding healing for our brokenness, both separately and then together, so that we are free to bury the baggage once and for all, and learn to love with an honesty, generosity and mutual acceptance which doesn't come easily to human beings of either gender?

THE PAIN OF PRETENCE

Writer Adrian Plass has become well-known for his gentle satire. He manages to give us a glimpse of what lies behind the super-spiritual, super-competent, super-dishonest masks we all hold so close in case reality catches us out.

The Real Problem

Sunday is a funny day,
It starts with lots of noise.
Mummy rushes round with socks,
And Daddy shouts, 'You boys!'

Then Mummy says, 'Now don't blame them,
You know you're just as bad,
You've only just got out of bed,
It really makes me mad!'

My mummy is a Christian,
My daddy is as well,
My mummy says, 'Oh heavens!'
My daddy says, 'Oh, hell!'

And when we get to church at last
It's really very strange,
Cos Mum and Dad stop arguing,
And suddenly they change.

At church my mum and dad are friends,
They get on very well,
But no one knows they've had a row,
And I'm not going to tell.

People often come to them,
Because they seem so nice,
And Mum and Dad are very pleased
To give them some advice.

They tell them Christian freedom
Is worth an awful lot,
But I don't know what freedom means,
If freedom's what they've got.

Daddy loves the meetings,
He's always at them all,
He's learning how to understand
The letters of Saint Paul.

But Mummy says, 'I'm stuck at home
To lead my Christian life,
It's just as well for blinkin' Paul
He didn't have a wife.'

I once heard Mummy say
She'd walk out of his life,
I once heard Daddy say to her
He'd picked a rotten wife.

They really love each other,
I really think they do.
I think the people in the church
Would help them – if they knew.

Adrian Plass

But the church may inadvertently add to the pressure. Communications consultant Peter Meadows worked for the Evangelical Alliance, is a member of the Spring Harvest Executive Committee, and was formerly the Chief Executive of Premier, the London Christian radio station. In his book Pressure Points, *writing about his wife's severe depression and his own subsequent burn-out, he said, 'I have become convinced that our churches contain vast numbers of people who would be deeply ashamed if their fellow Christians knew just how hopeless, helpless and overwhelmed they felt.'*

She was wearing a pink and white overall, had long blond hair, and more make-up on than most Christian women at that time – but she wasn't tarty. When we spoke it was her vulnerability which really touched me. We were both working for a Cliff Richard gospel concert in Manchester, I was on publicity, she was involved with the make-up. And that was how it all started.

Rosemary was an incredibly well-organized woman, juggling a home, five children, a catering company, and umpteen church commitments with the minimum of effort – the sort of person who if she had an early start in the morning, had her toothpaste on the brush the night before. Perhaps I should have seen the signs, but I didn't.

She had recovered so well from cancer of the thyroid after our fourth child was born that I couldn't see why there should be any more problems. Admittedly the surgeon's bedside manner had all the charm of napalm, but it was over, wasn't it?

She was taking antidepressants for six months before I knew anything about it. Her friends knew. She had confided in them. But not in me. Why couldn't she tell me? I felt threatened, isolated and betrayed. A whole part of her history and taken place without me. It took me a while to realize she felt guilty that she couldn't cope, afraid of being a burden to me, and ashamed of being unable to snap out of it.

My vivacious, outgoing companion vanished almost overnight. She became difficult, distant, couldn't bear me to touch her. Ordinary, everyday pressures turned into major traumas. 'You don't understand.' 'You don't care.' I was always wrong, whatever I did, confronting an issue or avoiding it. She was irrational, unreasonable. Someone with depressive illness sees the world through very distorted glasses – and that's hard if you happen to be close to them.

I adjusted my lifestyle. For four years I couldn't come home late for work, or stay away overnight. I couldn't even have five minutes of peace and privacy alone with my thoughts while I shaved, but left the bathroom door open, listening for the next crisis. Yes, I did resent being the one to make the compromises, cancel the meetings, sacrifice my career, while Rosemary went on catering. Yet I felt a heel. I knew she needed the work to help her survive, to give her a sense of normality, of achievement.

The church was no help. In fact it was disaster. I had a wife who was ill, five small children to care for – and they still expected me to be at the Sunday evening service, and fully committed to its punitive schedule of meetings. And why do Christians look down their noses at someone whose emotions crack, yet rally in sympathy when the problem is physical?

I ran on empty for far too long, and finally ended up being sent home from Spring Harvest by my colleagues in a state of utter exhaustion. 'Your lights were on, but there was nobody at home', one of them said later. It's hard for a man to fail. He wants to succeed, be in control. I felt as if my credibility as a Christian was severely threatened. But whatever I felt, I knew God hadn't moved, and being told to rest was the best thing that could have happened to us. We began at last to understand the problem, to see stress for what it was, to admit our inability to cope without blaming and beating ourselves. What a release to know we didn't have to play at being 'the perfect mother' or 'the perfect Christian man' any more. We employed someone to help with the children. We created time and space for each other, and began, slowly and painfully, to rebuild our broken lives.

Peter Meadows

Not every couple finds a way of working through their pain together. There is the man who appears to be blind to his own insensitivity and lack of feeling, and may even see it as an acceptable sign of his macho-ness.

Three Rounds with an Amateur Tyrant

Round One: From the bell he's after her. An upright bear, hopping from one pad to another. He tries a glancing head-swipe of 'You always say that'. She covers her face and staggers back. The ropes become her fragile cradle. No marks yet, but inside her a trickling haemorrhage of confusion seeps.

Round Two: She leaves her corner, a trouper. They clinch in which he sends her gum-shield flying. Her knees buckle, he backs off, satisfied. His point of view, the only point of view, is heard.

Round Three: Another clash; she crumples. The towel of silent withdrawal is thrown in. This makes him seethe and pummel her more. Being the referee as well, he allows this. Afterwards, in the First Aid Room, he visits her and says sorry. She cannot hear, he has beaten her deaf.

Stewart Henderson

Emotional wounds, despite their pain, are unseen. Not so with physical abuse, which is largely a male prerogative. When American writer Phyllis Alsdurf began preparing an article on domestic violence for the magazine, Christian Life Today, *she was shocked at what she found. 'As we have worked in this area we have felt outrage that violence of this sort occurs as frequently as it does in Christian homes and that it so often goes unchallenged by the church. In fact, the church has at times contributed to the mistreatment of women through complacency, insensitivity and its imbalanced teachings on male-female roles.'*

A survey on battered wives by Family *magazine (now* Parentwise) *in 1985 found that domestic violence was alive and kicking on this side of the Atlantic. Many of those who replied were married to men who held positions of responsibility in the church. 'He has read the Bible daily for twenty years,' said one woman, 'but for all the goodness he seems to pick up he might as well read* Playboy.' *Almost all found that the church let them down. 'All along the line, though they were loving and caring, they tell me that it's me that's wrong; if I reacted in a right way he wouldn't have to resort to this.'*

Few books have left me feeling as brutalized as Battered into Submission, *which gave me a glimpse into the dark and hellish world of women who had been kicked, beaten, bruised and dragged along the floor by their hair. By monsters? No, by ordained ministers, Christian businessmen and church leaders, the men who smile at us from the pulpit or sit next to us in the pew.*

After my marriage my husband treated me as a nonperson with no value other than through him. He cited Scripture passages in support of his treatment of me. Any time I objected to his behaviour or to his decisions, he told me that I was to submit to him just as totally as if he were Jesus Christ. He firmly believed that if I were obedient and submissive, God himself would take care of me. Therefore he was free to behave as irresponsibly as he liked without fear of hurting me or our child. He felt God wouldn't allow us to be hurt unless it was God's will.

My husband took no responsibility for his actions at all. I spent many agonizing hours in prayer and fasting, seeking to drive out every vestige of sin from my life. I believed that when I finally learned what God was trying to teach me, my husband would respond with love. But the more I submitted to him, the more arrogantly he displayed his flagrant abusive behaviour. I sought counsel from pastors and friends. Many didn't believe me. It's not hard to understand why. How could such an upstanding member of the church and community be capable of such a miscarriage of God's justice?

I despised his attendance and eager participation at church because it underlined the contrast to his behaviour at home. Those who did believe me offered no solace; only sympathy and empty platitudes. They affirmed my submissive reaction to my husband's abusive tyranny. No one at any time went to talk to my husband about his behaviour in loving correction. I was always left empty-handed to return to my personal hell.

James Alsdurf and Phyllis Alsdurf

THE PAIN OF FORBIDDEN LOVE

What makes a perfectly happily-married, church-going, middle-aged man or woman do what they have always found hard to understand in others, fall headlong in love with someone other than their spouse? Professor Cary Cooper at UMIST, who researches the psychology of work, says that it happens to men when their ego needs stroking, when they hunger for fresh reassurance. And women are by no means immune.

As soon as a husband feels that his wife has superimposed her moral diagnosis upon him, from which nothing can budge her, all true openness, all deep expression of himself, dries up. It may then happen that this husband will begin to speak with some girl he meets at the office or the sports club. He will open up easily to her about many things which he no longer dares to tell his wife. He will rediscover then the wonderful feeling for which every human being hungers, that of being understood. He will perhaps even speak to her of his marital problems. Men easily soften a woman's heart by means of their marriage disappointments. In my office this husband will possibly say, 'I cannot live without that young woman. She understands me, while my wife does not.' Tragedy is fast approaching!

Paul Tournier

Society dictates that we must follow our hearts, not our wills. The dictates of love must be obeyed, and love clamours for sexual gratification. But what if love's demands contradict the seventh commandment, who then should be obeyed?

'Sheila', who lives in the Midlands, decided she could not do what was clearly forbidden, but it was difficult and extremely painful decision. 'The second time I fell in love with another human being I was in my mid-forties. Falling in love was wonderful, amazing – and absolutely devastating. I wanted to tell the world how I felt, but simultaneously I was weighed down by guilt. I was middle-aged, respectably, solidly, and even happily married, responsibly employed and a committed and active member of the Church of England. I still am all these things. The experience of falling in love hit me like a thunderbolt out of the blue, and I knew that I could never be the same again, but I felt that I had a choice to make. Either I could let my feelings of guilt tear me apart and work destructively within my Christian life, or I could accept the gift of love as a blessing to enrich it.'

If God is love
does that mean my love for you,
and yours for me,
is all part of God?
Sometimes it feels like that –
when I catch your eye
and feel affection exchanged,
or laugh with you
or, understanding,
feel myself understood.
Sometimes I love you so much
there's no room in me for anything else!
Do you ever feel like that about me?

Sometimes, though,
when I can't see you,
my love for you is destructive.
It tears me apart.
I want you with me;
I need to touch you.
If we were together then
and you felt the same
we would make love
and regret it afterwards.
Would God be in that, too?

If wanting you is wrong,
does that mean my love is wrong, as well?
To love you
yet not to express it
explodes in pain;
the thought of shutting out love
is unendurable.
I have no choice but to love.

Something in you
calls to the depths in me.
God help me to respond to you without sin,
and you to respond to me.

'Could my experience of human love enable me to love God more fully?' That was the question Sheila asked herself. Yes, was her answer, but she also knew it would not have been, had she not resisted the temptation to sexual gratification and the guilt which would have ensued.

Adultery, in the mind or with the body, has a destructive effect on the innocent partner who is suddenly shut out from the relationship which is theirs by right. How do they cope with such a basic betrayal?

'Sarah' is married to a well-known preacher and church leader. For years he had loved her through her struggle to find inner wholeness and healing. Then, when at last she felt able to respond, she was forced to confront a terrible irony, that his love for her had somehow shrivelled in the process.

A Husband's Infatuation

Too painful for tears
Shocked and paralysed
Too painful to think
Numbed unbelief.

Gradually the truth entered my mind
Short sharp bursts of painful reality
Then out again as soon as they
had touched my consciousness.

Physical pain and retching
I held my stomach for comfort
But there was no relief from the agonizing ache
Only sleep tablets to forget for a few hours.

Then the tears came
Floods and floods and floods.
This can't be happening to me
But it is.

Thank God for his words of life.
Thank friends for their listening ear.
Thank pain that it will bring
its own fruitfulness.

Until then O God
Keep me from evil and despair
Keep me in truth and love
Learning to be calm and patient.

*Sarah and her husband go on painfully working at their rela-
tionship. Richard Kell was forced to abandon the one he writes
about here. Born in Youghal, Co. Cork, the son of a Methodist
missionary and the widower of the poem, he retired in 1983 from
his final teaching post as senior lecturer in English Literature at
the Newcastle-upon-Tyne Polytechnic, now University of
Northumbria. He had four children, but his eldest son died in
1995. As well as contributing to many anthologies, he has
published five books of poetry, including* Rock and Water.

*This poem, about his relationship with a divorcee, describes
how difficult it was for her to trust a man the second time*

around. It touched in him all the uncertainty men feel about their maleness, the pain it engenders, and their longing for the intimacy with woman they knew with their mothers.

The Divorcee and the Widower

Cool, guarded, she weighs him up. At least
that's what she thinks she's doing, but in fact
he's in the make-up chair; a standard Beast
is forming at her touch – the eyebrows blacked
and spread like raven wings, a shadowed stare
recalling one that drove her to despair.

Now every word he offers will attest
his patriarchal guilt. Her programmed brain
Is satisfied that he's 'like all the rest' –
male-chauvenistic, lustful, selfish, vain.
He's trapped: for how would silence, or a smile,
go down in her interrogation file?

Though monster, he supports all human rights,
and therefore women's – can even understand
why, made for popes and merchants, kings and knights,
expressions long in service are unmanned.
No wonder there's a boom in lesbian love
and heteromanticism gets the shove.

The trouble is – well, isms. Where they rise,
new dogmas and constraints replace the old.
He hints at such misgivings, but her eyes
assure him that the effort leaves her cold.
Then, in a pause, her image disappears
and memory floats him back across the years.

He sees a devil-husband, one who dips
small bottoms and vaginas in the suds,
with creamy spoonfuls coaxes blobby lips,
shakes baby talc on penises like buds;
who digs, repairs, paints walls and windowsills,
holds down a stressful job to meet the bills.

What have we done to ourselves? Years of tautness,
a gaucheness hiding its face behind our ritual,
a coil and wriggle in ourselves we want to veil.
Look! how those women caress and touch with ease.
Sisters, sisters, it's us you're trying to free;
more than your scorn, our dealer's grope needs pity.

And weren't you women once those mothers drying
up our tears? A face shown and withdrawn.
Slugs and snails and puppy dogs. *Stand like a man.*
Tell me, did you ever see your father crying?
A coin's faces, each a keeper for the other.
Woman and man, somehow we're in this together.

Richard Kell

HEALING FOR THE PAIN

The painful feeling of being 'shut out' seems a common experience to both men and women. Women often talk about being shut out from the male world of work and sport, while men complain that childbirth, or women's health issues, or their emotional trauma leave them standing on the sidelines. It is part of the human condition that when we need each other the most, we tend to retreat into ourselves. Perhaps we feel it is enough to have to cope with our own pain, let alone someone

171

else's. Martyn Green's experience of his wife's breast cancer highlights how helpless men can feel when they cannot reach their loved one, or solve her problem, how quick to blame themselves. But perhaps that's a vital part of the healing process.

Original Sin

When I first felt your body
shudder and shake with what
the news might be;
I silently asked
was this dread caused by having to
cope with responsibilities which were
not yours alone;
or by the stress of a relationship made
heavy by years of neglect;
or by the subjugation of your own being –
a loss of wildness, freedom and eventually more
or
was your cancer really caused by me,
once again offering the bittersweet
fruit of blame?

Martyn Green

Vicar of Chew Magna with Dundry in the Bath and Wells Diocese, Melvyn Matthews was previously Director of the Ammerdown Retreat Centre and Senior Chaplain at Bristol University. He calls himself 'an occasional poet', and wrote the following poem for his wife, after a disaster with one of their children. It was he who suggested I include a category on the pain of loving, 'for those of us who want to be new men, but find it hard'.

The First Things

I come late again to the first things,
the first loves I had abandoned
thoughtlessly, thinking them slight or
womanish, fey or spare.

I come late again to the first things,
the things I left for the heights of mind,
the views from the towers of complexity and the
quest for an elegant solution.

I left them behind
and took up with others, who
wielded me, caught me strong, giving
identity in grief or a winding sheet
for my loneliness

But now that grief again has undone me,
now I know what I nearly lost,
now, slowly, like dark whales they rise
to the surface of my life, and blow
Their rain across my dryness.

They stand like great beeches in summer,
breathing slowly on the hillside in evening,
Quiet and waiting, calling my name.

These rich silences have waited
for my return. They are the soul friends
who were drowned,
wounded, almost lost in the darkness of desires.
They reach out for me.

She too has waited, patiently bleeding,
looking darkly with love – a love I have
trifled, troubled, fought with too much.

But now in the dark
I shake with great thankfulness
and call for them all with joy
laughing at my homecoming

Melvin Matthews

Whether deliberately or by neglect, men, it seems, have inflicted immense pain on women. But men can also be the key to their healing. Whether they hurt women further, or exercise a ministry of love, nurture and support, seems proportionate to the measure of healing they themselves have received from Jesus Christ, the only man perfectly at ease with his maleness. This is an excerpt from the Henry Martyn lecture given by Elaine Storkey to the Evangelical Missionary Alliance in 1994.

Where are the men at the end of the century? Is the Christian man open to the leading of God? Or is he stuck in secularism, competitiveness, individualism and egocentricity? For there is much pride in today's Christian man. It is difficult enough for men to see themselves as nurturers and supportive fathers in this present climate, let alone to let go of some of their privileges, even some of their leadership, power and potential.

Here's a challenge for them: let them imagine what it's like to be a woman, especially women of a few decades ago who were involved in missionary work. How did it feel to serve overseas for many years, come home and never be allowed to use the calling and gifts God had given? Only when we put ourselves in another's shoes do we experience what many women have known: the longing to serve God, even knowing the gifting of God, yet being discarded because of their sex.

If there is to be greater openness in the church only men can bring it about. Men alone can let go of the power they assumed was theirs and take on the humility of Christ. For women alone to fight for their own rights is to move away from the servant heart of Christ. The whole body of Christ must come together and lay down power, pride, prestige and privilege so that they can be shared out equally.

The Christian man needs to stand against the pressures and direction of a culture in which television and the advertising media reinforce powerful images of what it is to be a man: to be competitive, vying for supremacy, making sure women don't gain the upper hand. Instead he is invited to be the one to break the mould, to bring peace and mutuality to the new woman, hope and healing to the suffering woman, empathy and a listening ear to the angry woman. In my work with women who are incest survivors it is very often Christian men who can break the hold of the past, when they offer ordinary relationships with no hidden agenda. The challenge for Christian men is to treat Christian women as sisters, co-workers worthy of respect, with gifts and callings that should be recognised and honoured before God.

Elaine Storkey

11

Vive la Différence

Men charge into things without thinking, and leave us to work out the practicalities and implications of their actions.

Serena Lailey, headteacher's wife

For a man production is measured in the quantity of things produced, but for a woman, in the enjoyment of their use.

Paul Tournier

Every child soon learns what makes little boys different from little girls. It's obvious. Or is it? Perhaps the so-called facts of life we teach them are too basic. It's only when we look beyond the obvious that we begin to see how radically different we are, more different than I realized when I started this compilation, frighteningly so. There were times when I began to wonder how two people of the opposite sex ever manage to go on living or working together. And other times I marvelled at the miracle that we do and that God organized it that we should.

If he ever goes bald, my son's head will look like a patch-work quilt, it has been stitched together so often. I felt like putting up a camp-bed in the local hospital's casualty department when he was a toddler. He had no sense of danger, or if he had, it was an attraction, not a caution. He simply rushed headlong into the next project without a thought. His sister, on the other hand, while never demure or unadventurous, would usually think about the significance of her actions before she left our side.

As we get older, little seems to change. Take, for example, the relationship between a man and his car. He pushes, bullies, takes out all his aggression on this subservient metal box. That's why sexy women are used to advertise them. 'You may not be able to master her, guys, but you can master the car.' Men have more fatal accidents and kill more children on the roads. They feel in control and don't give a thought for the human factor. Women tend to drive more carefully. They say to themselves, 'A child could run out of that drive.'

Several months ago my husband narrowly escaped being killed in a car crash. A lorry driver had failed to see his little red Corsa join the motorway, and moved swiftly and inexorably over into his lane, garrotting him between a concrete wall on his left and the thunderous, sixty-mile-an-hour juggernaut on his right. We were both quite shocked, even though I wasn't in the car – but our reactions were totally different. Peter was terrified by his loss of control. All I could say was, 'How couldn't the lorry driver see you? Why didn't he have adequate mirrors? Why didn't he think of the consequences?'

Male drive and female prudence, things versus people, but it isn't quite that simple. Where would women be without men who throw caution to the wind in the name of passion? 'Dairy Box Man' lives, the incurable romantic risking his all for his mate. 'On the other hand', says my friend, Serena, 'if Julian came home having booked a romantic weekend in Paris, you can be sure he wouldn't have left me time to organize the child-minding, or pack.'

We need and complement each other. Men may be competitive, but beware female rivalry. As Paul Tournier knows, from his experience of counselling mothers-in-law, women can abuse their relational talents if it suits them and justify their jealousies. And it may take a man to see it.

The secret of enjoying our differences is respecting the otherness of the opposite sex. Men haven't always been very good at that, perhaps because they're not used to seeing themselves as men. Roy McCloughry says, 'There is an inequality between men and women in that while women are acutely aware of themselves as women, men are invisible to themselves as men.' Only when we appreciate the qualities inherent in our own gender, can we appreciate each other. 'Self-awareness is an essential part of that self-control which is one of the hallmarks of a mature Christian character. It is an essential part of a journey towards being able to love others and act justly. But if some men are unwilling even to undertake this journey then they condemn themselves to being stunted spiritually.' Women too are spiritually diminished when we refuse to face up to the weaknesses of our own sex.

It's not difficult to major on our misunderstandings, the way we bring each other irritation and aggravation, but what about the stimulation, inspiration or just plain comfort? Ultimately we would be hopelessly lost without each other. We were created different – for each other. Long live our differences! They present us with a constant challenge.

Throughout his ministry Jesus appears to have been better understood by the women in his life. They were there for him in the times of crisis, even when the men had slunk away or fallen asleep. He seemed to enjoy their 'otherness'.

Why are there more women than men in the church? Because men are more rational and practical, women instinctively more spiritual? Not necessarily so. Here Hugh Montefiore, Bishop of Birmingham from 1978–1987, explores one or two possible answers to this difficult, yet very important question.

The Churching of Women

Feminists in the church have been so concerned with getting women to the altar that they have largely ignored the question posed by the preponderance of women in the pew. Anyone who attends church or chapel cannot fail to be struck that there are always far more women present than men.

This is not merely an Anglican phenomenon: it is found equally in Roman Catholic, Orthodox and Free Church congregations (although less perhaps in independent chapels and house fellowships). Surveys show that there is the same mismatch in believing as in belonging: women believe more than men and in a greater proportion than men. What is more, they pray more in private than men.

No one has ever explained really satisfactorily why this should be so. Sociologists suggest that women tend to think of God in terms of love, comfort, forgiveness, while men naturally picture him in terms of power and control. But I don't see why that should make women more religious. Is there a fundamental difference between the sexes, or now that women are achieving the same status as men, will the difference begin to even out?

Many theories have been adduced to explain women's religiosity. Some are psychological, concerned with guilt or anxiety, or God as a father figure (although I am not clear why women should react differently in these matters from men). Some are compensation theories, suggesting that women's status and lack of opportunities, compared with men tends to make them more religious. It is certainly true that women find it easier than men to get down on their knees and pray, and perhaps their former, more lowly status helps them. I don't think that it's likely to be sublimated sexuality that tends to make spinsters religious: there's plenty of repressed sexuality in males, but it doesn't do that.

A third type of theory explains the difference in terms of the roles women play in society, often involving self-sacrifice, as in child-rearing and caring for others. None of these is entirely satisfactory.

Perhaps the true explanation is a combination of these theories. Perhaps there is a genetic explanation. Female brains, we are told, have evolved differently from those of the male gender: perhaps a greater development of the right hemisphere makes them more open to the transcendant. Until we know the answers, men are unlikely to be attracted into church in the same proportion as women.

Hugh Montefiore

I'm not convinced that it's all a matter of nature, not nurture. Paul Tournier has another, interesting suggestion to throw into the pot.

Even Our Consciences Are Different!

The man is in general more conscious of his sins than the woman is of hers. He is very conscious of his sexual lust, of his lying to his wife, or to his competitor, of his cheating on income tax, or of his excessive pride in his work. Perhaps this is one reason why he goes to church less willingly than his wife. He feels less at ease there. He feels a little pharisaical in thus publicly parading his piety, for he very well knows what is not right in his real life and what he does not feel capable of setting right. . . .

Women are generally less conscious of their sins. Take jealousy for example. A woman can persecute her daughter-in-law most atrociously without the least recognition that she is being driven by her jealousy. She would be deeply hurt if you were to tell her so. Quite the contrary, she is fully persuaded that she is acting out of love. It is out of love for her son, and also for her daughter-in-law, she thinks, that she scolds her for those shortcomings she sees, and tries to correct them. She wants them to be happy! She can listen to moving sermons on love and be stirred by them without the smallest twinge of conscience. . . . Perhaps this is one reason why there are so many women with countless scruples, seeking to discover small sins since they are oblivious of the other ones.

Paul Tournier

Conscience, culture, brain-function, so many possible basic differences between men and women. 'Civilisation built by men', according to Tournier, 'would remain abstract, cold, technical and dehumanised'. But not, according to Evangeline Paterson, as long as there are gentle old academics like her husband in the world. In this affectionate portrait of her husband in

*retirement we meet a breed of man whose calm, regular habits,
whose ease with life and with themselves, bring a special kind
of tranquillity into the space they inhabit.*

Civilisation

Saturday afternoon. Professor Paterson
walks in his garden, bends on his daffodils
looks fond yet stern. His brain, unoccupied, idles.
He hums. Half-heartedly, the watery sun
attempts to gild him, like a saint. He moves
away, deeply ponders a hole in the fence,
reproves a dangling creeper.

    His wife, in the kitchen,
scours the pans. The radio chatters calamity.
Civilisation is teetering to a fall.
Music erupts, with thud and boom and crash
– the mangonels* of the last assault? She sluices
water around the sink. She drops a cup.
Its shatters.

    Professor Paterson
sits in his usual chair, and reads. Daffodils
stand in a vase behind him. He looks kindly
over his spectacles. The world settles
back on its base.
    Civilisation, it seems,
Is with us yet. She goes to make him tea.

mangonel = a military engine for casting stones

Evangeline Paterson

*Some women instinctively prefer the company of men, and feel
more at home in a traditional male world.*

*Teacher Ann Gager deliberately opted for secondary, rather
than primary school posts, knowing she was likely to have more
male colleagues. Now the mother of four girls, there is nothing
she would like more than to be confronted with four sets of
muddy football boots.*

A Woman's Best Friend

My first friends were boys. Growing up with two elder
brothers meant that my first adventures, first experiments,
first baring of the soul was with boys.

As I grew up I found the company of my brothers and
their friends preferable to that of my female school
friends. This was not because they were *the opposite sex*.
I don't think that even occurred to me. In fact, I couldn't
cope with girlie obsessions with boys: buying clothes to
attract them, experimenting with make-up to dazzle them,
with the ultimate goal of having one's own boyfriend. I
preferred being with boys no matter how I was dressed,
because I liked their sense of humour, their ability to laugh
in most circumstances and their capacity not to analyse
themselves or take themselves too seriously.

I left the lads at home and went off to college when I
was eighteen, to a hostel with twenty-two other females.
After about a week together, on Saturday at 4.40 pm, I
shouted, 'Quick, the TV.' Blank faces.

I thought that the excitement of coming to college
must have made them forget what day it was.

'It's Saturday', I said encouragingly.

No response.

'Football results.'

Not one of them was remotely interested. I was devastated. It was a strange and unhappy experience to realize I wasn't going to fit easily into a female habitat.

Sport has continued to be a great passion of mine, both to play and to watch. It was after a hockey match that I was paid the greatest of compliments by a man. 'You're the only woman I've ever gone into a shoulder tackle with . . . and come off worst.'

Now, taking a break in my teaching career, I find myself the mother of four daughters (ironic, isn't it?) and am largely thrust again into a female world with other mothers. I manage, but don't think I am at my happiest. Having a husband brings many compensations. It means spending some of every day with my favourite male friend. It means having someone with whom I can share my love of God and Manchester United.

Recently, when Manchester United was playing a vital championship game and I wanted to watch it with the lads, guess who had the four children? Yes, because he's male and understands how important these things are.

Ann Gager

What else do women like about men? Personally, I'm rather fond of that testosterone drive of theirs, and just a little envious of the boyish enthusiasm which hurtles them on, without so much as a backward glance. Other women liked his familiar smell, his voice, a shoulder to cry on, or simply a strong masculine, 'I've-got-this-situation-in-control' presence. Most valued a man free enough to be himself and take the risk of expressing his real feelings.

A Man with His Skin Off

I spied a man
with his skin off: chilling
to watch him peel flayed flesh like
a child letting the doctor
see where it hurts

thrilling
into my nerve and soul sinew;
so rare
a man to walk
naked to windward
and grow, love, change, feel
like a real
human soul, like me
like a woman

Veronica Zundel

In the last section Elaine Storkey explained how men can bring healing to women. The reverse is also true. My personal feeling is that the time has perhaps come when women can help deliver men from their innate loneliness and isolation.

Open His Cage

We're inundated with women's writings on being a woman. But why do so few men wax lyrical about the joys, the struggles, the pain of being a man? They don't really grouse about the pressure of juggling a full-time job, church commitment and running a family. They don't fly the flag for better preventative measures against prostate cancer. They barely mention the effects of their hormones (not in public at any rate, though my husband moans about them every time he looks at his ever-receding hairline in the mirror).

At the risk of being extremely patronizing, and it may of course simply be my female way of looking at it, I think it must be hard to be a man. Imagine the strain of living with all those expectations: to be the provider, to be competent, to be a leader, to be strong, to succeed. For them no access to instant brotherhood, sharing recipes, wingeing about the way her snoring keeps him awake at night, moaning about holes in their socks, giggling about the predictability of the opposite sex, having a good natter – in the Gents.

My husband and three other men went off together in the car the other evening to a rather turgid, compulsory church service. Peter arrived home at 8.30 p. m. alone.

'What are you doing back so soon?' I asked him.

'Well, the service was over early', he said.

'So why didn't the four of you go and have a drink together somewhere?'

'But we don't know each other', he said.

'You might, if you spent time together.'

What he meant was they had no interests in common, no activities they could share. Four women would have needed no excuse to go and have a drink together, except the pleasure of each other's company.

An inherent loneliness is built into the male gender, the fruits of a patriarchal society where men are supposed to be powerful and competent, and admitting any emotion is a sign of weakness. In orthodox Judaism, which is a matriarchal system, men fare a little better, though not much. Though the entire responsibility for prayer and religious leadership rests upon male shoulders, any Jewish woman will tell you who the boss is. The point is he must never find out. He needs to think he's in charge, or he might have a crisis of confidence.

While Jewish men thank God they're not a woman, I thank God I'm not a man. Cultural expectations force men into a cage and lock the door on them, despite the New Testament being full of men who were vulnerable yet strong. Jesus cried. Peter failed. John was tender. Paul hurt. None were ashamed of their feelings. And they found the sort of close and loving male friendships which many men can only dream of today.

So now girls, it's up to us. Shall we leave them in the cage, or, shall we take our men by the hand, be they friend, colleague, son or spouse, and gently coax them out into a new-found freedom?

Michele Guinness

Singer Tammy Wynette, explaining why she wrote the song, 'Stand by Your Man', said a woman knows her man will do all kinds of ridiculous things, but she loves him despite that, and will give him strength when he needs it. Her love and support, the sense of security and acceptance she gives, these were all qualities men valued in their women. What else do they like about us? Here's a random selection of comments I received:

Everything. Men do become attracted to the physical things first – a pretty face, figure, tight jeans, baggy jumper, confidence . . . but that's just the beginning.

I like the way women find men attractive.

I find chatty, sparky women fun, women who enjoy life.
It makes up for my rather dour outlook on life.

I enjoy women's thoughtfulness and sensitivity.

I like the way women appreciate each other. 'Hasn't she
lovely hair?' 'Isn't she pretty?' If I said that about another
man all my male friends would stand with their backs to
the wall and hastily talk in deep voices about rugby.

I like the way women can touch and hold each other,
without people thinking they are lesbians.

I envy women for being able to carry babies.

*And sometimes he loves her simply for being her. She affirms
his maleness, and turns the ordinary into something sacred,
something to celebrate.*

*Robert Siegel, Professor of English at the University of
Wisconsin – Milwaukee, has won awards for his poems. 'For
me,' he says, 'poetry is one way of apprehending the reality that
underlies and inhabits our world.' This poem ends with a ref-
erence to his wife, Ann, and arose out of 'a peculiarly intense
feeling of wonder at the mundane'.*

A Song of Praises

    for the gray nudge of dawn at the window
    for the chill that hangs around the bed and slips
        its cold tongue under the covers

for the cat who walks over my face purring murderously
for the warmth of the hip next to mine and sweet
    lethargy
for the cranking up of the will until it turns me out
    of bed
for the robe's warm caress along arm and shank
for the welcome of hot water, the dissolving of
       the night's stiff mask in the soft washcloth
for the light along the white porcelain sink
for the toothbrush's savory invasion of the tomb of the
    mouth
       and the resurrection of the breath
for the warm lather and the clean scrape of the razor
       and the skin smooth and pink that emerges
for the steam of the shower, the apprehensive shiver
    and then
        its warm enfolding of the shoulders
        its falling on the head like grace
        its anointing of the whole body
        and the soap's smooth absolution
for the rough nap of the towel and its message to each
    skin cell
for the hairbrush's pulling and pulling, waking the
    root of each hair
for the reassuring snap of elastic
for the hug of the belt that pulls all together
for the smell of coffee rising up the stairs announcing
    paradise
for the glass of golden juice in which light is condensed
       and the grapefruit's sweet flesh
       for the incense of butter on toast
        for the eggs, like twin peaks over which the sun
        rises
        and the jam for which the strawberries of summer
        have

saved themselves
for the light whose long shaft lifts the kitchen into the
   realms of day
for Mozart elegantly measuring out the gazebos of
   heaven on the radio
and for her face, for whom the kettle sings, the coffee
   percs,
      and all the yellow birds in the wallpaper spread
      their wings.

Robert Siegel

*The former poet laureate John Betjeman (1906–84) also felt
that there was something about a woman which could enable
a man to come face to face with his God, if only he allowed and
celebrated the feelings she inspired, rather than banish them to
some inner closet.*

Lenten Thoughts of a High Anglican

Isn't she lovely, 'the Mistress'?
With her wide-apart grey-green eyes,
The droop of her lips and, when she smiles,
Her glance of amused surprise?

How nonchalantly she wears her clothes,
How expensive they are as well!
And the sound of her voice is as soft and deep
As the Christ Church tenor bell.

But why do I call her 'the Mistress'
Who knows not her way of life?
Because she has more of a cared-for air
Than many a legal wife.

How elegantly she swings along
In the vapoury incense veil,
The Angel choir must pause in song
When she kneels at the altar rail.

The preacher said that we should not stare
Around when we come to Church,
Or the Unknown God we are seeking
May forever elude our search.

And I hope that the preacher will not think
It unorthodox and odd
If I add that I catch in 'the Mistress'
A glimpse of the Unknown God.

John Betjeman

Over twenty years ago, son of a Governor-General of Canada and Dartmouth-trained naval officer, Jean Vanier invited three handicapped young men to share his home. From one little old house in the village of Trosly-Breuil near Paris, to over seventy communities all over the world, representing two hundred homes for the mentally handicapped, the story of L'Arche is fast becoming a contemporary legend. After twenty years' experience, Vanier has discovered that when it comes to the deep inner yearning of man for woman and woman for man, there is very little difference between mentally handicapped people and every other human being. The fragility, the vulnerability of every heart that reaches out in love is the same. Emotional maturity is never achieved overnight. It has to be worked at and worked out carefully, taking full account of Christian and community values. But in the end it is a relationship which has the capacity to bring more joy than any other.

A milieu with both men and women is the best and truest one for someone with a mental handicap. The woman calls forth in the man that which is most profound: the heart, tenderness and sensitivity. The man thus becomes more gentle, more attentive, more discerning. He opens himself more to others. The woman awakens his goodness, just as the man awakens all that is most beautiful and feminine in the woman. Man and woman are as mirrors to each other; their differences reveal to each other who he or she is. They permit each one to be himself or herself in his masculinity or femininity. In a mixed milieu, work must be shared according to tastes and aptitudes; men and women more naturally find their own place and, through that, assume a clearer responsibility.

Jean Vanier

Strictly speaking, the following poem by psychiatrist A. S. J. Tessimond hasn't anything to do with the way women and men feel about each other. But it does seem to provide a vital clue in the mystery of how we begin to chip away at years of misunderstanding and fear. Fear is the bully in our lives. It drives us into all kinds of inappropriate behaviour. It locks us into our hurts and resentments. Only when we confront it, examine it, and understand where it comes from, do we remove its power to tyrannize and imprison us. Then, face to face with our true selves are we able to reach out, fearlessly, and appreciate the otherness of those we love.

The Psychiatrist's Song

Learn to know the mind-behind-
Mind that sees when you are blind.
Learn to trust the mind below-
Mind that's wiser than you know.

Learn to meet the fear you fear,
Hate you hate, and see them clear.
Enter the forbidden place.
Face at last your other face.

Learn to be alone; then only
Reach out hand no longer lonely.
Grow, be tall yet reconciled
To yourself, the weeping child.

Love; be easy, and be warm.
Find the fire beyond the form.
Laugh. Forgive yourself: forgive
Sins long dead, and learn to live.

A. S. J. Tessimond

12

Without You

I love thee with a love I seemed to lose
With my lost saints – I love thee with the breath,
Smiles, tears, all of my life! – and if God choose,
I shall but love thee better after death.

Elizabeth Barrett Browning (1806–61)

The attraction that man and woman have for each other
calls them to go beyond another isolation: death.

Jean Vanier

Perhaps we never truly appreciate each other, until we lose one
another. After the death of her husband, my mother-in-law
said that what she missed most of all was his arms. She could
look back and laugh at the difficulties, the hurts, the things
that had maddened her intensely. Suddenly they no longer
mattered. Now there was no one to hold her or touch her, as
he had done.

There's 'a time to lose' according to the writer of Ecclesiastes, though most of us prefer not to dwell on it and live as if
it wasn't the case. If we did, we might take our relationships a

little less for granted, see them in their finite proportions, struggle a little less. Without loss what we have is never put to the test.

There is a terrible finality about death, which brings down the curtain on our human performance, but is that the end of the drama? Of course, not every man or woman relishes the thought of continuing above what they didn't enjoy down here. 'Where do you think my husband's gone?' one widow asked my husband when he went to see her to discuss the funeral arrangements. 'Will we be re-united?' He stalled, not wanting to upset her. 'We don't know for certain', he said. 'Thank God', she said. 'It's been bad enough living with him here.'

But where there is deep love, it seems instinctive to long for relationships which are only temporarily postponed by the grave. Is human love part of the Christian's share in eternity? Some, since they have found it to be the nearest thing to heaven on this earth, think that it must be. Perhaps it isn't too much to believe that one day, restored to the garden, we shall join Adam and Eve, and revel together in the harmony which was our birthright, forfeited only for one small era in time.

No amount of social acceptance or understanding lessens the sense of personal failure which accompanies divorce. Divorce is a kind of bereavement, accompanied as it is by a sense of grief and loss, even if the relationship had been long since dead. Some would say it is worse than death because the partner lives, but becomes inaccessible, and may go on causing pain. It is certainly a denial of the happier days in a way death is not, a cruel hacking apart of two people who once were one.

Leaving You

'Take what you must have
    and go –'

A pair of sheets,
a kettle and a mug,
some records and a radio . . . I take what is mine
from what was ours,
dividing what cannot be shared,
deciding painfully
how to tear each thing,
without breaking,
bleeding.

How can one home become two
each single object halved,
a morsel for each.

So much between us, eternity between us
rage between us, where once was love.
How can I halve my heart
that once was given to you.

Jean Clark

*The ravages of war, bringing heartache, grief and separation,
have been the scourge of our history. If it is the lot of men to
cause and sustain them, it is the lot of women to sacrifice their
menfolk to them. Occasionally it is the other way round.*

*Najwa Farah was born in Nazareth to an Arab Christian
family. She was one of the very few girls to train as a teacher in
the Women's Training College in Jerusalem when Palestine was*

still subject to the British Mandate. In 1950 she married Rafiq Farah, an Anglican priest, and for the next thirty-five years they spent their time in Israel, on the West Bank, and in Beirut, trying to love and comfort the Arab Christian community through a time of immense turmoil and suffering.

Saffiyah

A pot of jasmine stood on a window sill
Its scent spread and livened Saffiyah's dreams
Who lived in a room, its roof is of scrap rusty tin
In the Palestine Camp in the Southern suburbs
Of unhappy Beirut.
Dreaming of her beloved who'd gone to defend them,
Of his handsome face, his strong fist
She is proud of him, enumerates to herself
His mighty deeds.
He attacked a tank, fought in the castle of Shaqeef.

She helps in the kitchen with other Palestinian women
To provide fighters a shared meal.
He watches her, carrying the loaves of bread
Shielding herself in the narrow alley
To where he and his companions will have their supper.

A phosphorous bomb falls, explodes,
And the alley and the room are destroyed
Saffiyah is torn to pieces, burnt.
He runs to carry the dismembered scorched body.

Alone he cries, kissing what was a cheek, a hand.
The scent of the jasmine spreads

From the fallen, broken pot.
It was spared, also a cat that wanders in the alleys
    of the camp.

He lays the jasmine on what is left of the body.
Evening falls.

The heavens shine
It is not Christmas Eve,
But those are the lit bombs,
Red, orange, dangling from the sky
Like great Christmas baubles.

Farewell Saffiyah,
Farewell my shattered dream.
It looks like Christmas Eve,
A Western Christmas Eve with gifts
To the children of Palestine.

Najwa Farah

C. S. Lewis was an Oxford don, renowned for his agnostic views, whose faith became the source of his popularity. He was the creator of a series of children's books, set in the allegorical land of Narnia, which delight children everywhere, though he never had children of his own; a chain-smoking Anglo-Catholic who married a Jewish American divorcee and is still regarded by evangelicals as one of the greatest Christian apologists of the century; an academic who said he couldn't understand how anyone could marry a woman since every topic of conversation would be used up in the first six months, then fell hopelessly in love with the most unlikely candidate for his affections, and found life almost impossible without her. Perhaps the paradoxes in Lewis' life are the source of his power. He was never anything if not honest about his struggles. When his wife Joy died of cancer, his frank admission of wretchedness and loss, the wrestling with his faith, and the ultimate resolution of it all, have brought comfort to the countless people who try to make sense of their own suffering.

'My heart and body are crying out, come back, come back . . . But I know this is impossible. I know that the thing I want I can never get. The old life, the jokes, the drinks, the arguments, the love-making, the tiny, heart-breaking commonplace . . .'

Joys that Sting

To take the old walks alone, or not at all,
To order one pint where I ordered two,
To think of, and then not to make, the small
Time-honoured joke (senseless to all but you);

To laugh (oh, one'll laugh), to talk upon
Themes that we talked upon when you were there,
To make some poor pretence of going on,
Be kind to one's old friends, and seem to care,

While no one (O God) through the years will say
The simplest, common word in just your way.

C. S. Lewis

Sylvia Hedinger, Wycliffe missionary in the Cameroon, was only forty-seven when she died. I met her first when I was seventeen, a fresher at Manchester University. She was the vice-president of the Christian Union, with a reputation for being 'spiritual'. On the one hand she was so single-minded about serving Christ she terrified me half to death. On the other, her wisdom and impish sense of humour made her company irresistible.

She was unusual for her time, a woman who never shirked from saying what she thought, no matter how unpalatable. Whenever I grumbled about how difficult life could be, she would say, 'You think you're greater than your master, do you? We're called to obey, not be happy.' You could never reply, 'Well, its all right for you . . .' because she lived what she said. A curate fell very much in love with her, and she with him. He wrote her an anguished letter begging her not to be a missionary. She could serve God just as well as a clergy wife. 'He's right of course,' she said, with a wistful twinkle in her eye, when we single girls tried to tell her she might never get a better offer, 'but I'm called to be a Wycliffe missionary, not a clergy wife.'

How overjoyed we all were when she met Robert Hedinger at the Wycliffe Training Centre. Theirs was a very fruitful marriage. The news of her death of a rare form of cancer, just over twenty years later, was like a punch in the stomach. Why, when there was so much for her and Robert still to do in the Cameroon? Why, when her two boys still needed their mother? Robert asks 'the big why' too, but also believes, in his pain, that he doesn't need to know the answers – just yet.

Tears

when I read
what you have been
to many friends

tears

when I ride
in the car
that took you last

tears

when I see
your face
in the prime of life

tears

when I go
where we have been
together

tears

when I announce
again and again
that you have died

tears

when they sing
'O when the saints
go marching in'

tears

when we'll be there
together
then

tears no more

Robert Hedinger

*The well-known Victorian preacher and writer, Henry Grattan
Guinness, scandalized polite evangelical society when he took
for his second wife a woman more than forty years his junior.
He was sixty-seven, and she twenty-six, and he loved her with
all the passion with which a man can love a woman, knowing,
how could he not, that their time together must be short. In the
event they had seven years, and managed to produce two sons,
when he was seventy and seventy-two. Irresponsible male
behaviour? Some might says so, but even in 1910 a determined
woman survived. Grace went out, found work and raised her
boys single-handed. But she chose not to remarry. It was as if
those seven years had given her more than enough love for one
lifetime. And perhaps, in the context of eternity, they were
merely a beginning, not an ending.*

One Forever

Love links the living with the dead,
  The dead who only are departed;
For lingering still when joys are fled
  Love binds around the broken-hearted
A sense of that which never dies
A tie that reaches to the skies.

For from beyond the shadowy veil
   Sweet voices cry, we love you still,
For heaven-born love can never fail,
   Or cease the holy heart to fill,
And souls that love are sundered never
But one on earth are one forever.

Henry Grattan Guinness

Sources and Acknowledgements

Introduction

Gordon Dalbey, *Healing the Masculine Soul* (Word Publishing 1988).

Come into the Garden, Maud

'Two of far nobler shape' by John Milton (1608–1674) from *Paradise Lost*, Book 1.

Quote by Mary Stewart van Leeuwen from *Gender and Grace* (IVP 1990).

'The Apple' by Lady Margaret Sackville (1881–1963), from *Faith in Her Words: Six Centuries of Women's Poetry*, compiled by Veronica Zundel (Lion 1991).

'Missing' by Stewart Henderson from *Homeland* (Hodder and Stoughton 1993).

'We are fired into life . . .' by Ronald Rolheiser from *Forgotten Among the Lilies* (Spire 1990).

'In Eden . . .' by Phyllis Trible from *God and the Rhetoric of Sexuality* (Philadelphia: Fortress Press 1978).

'When a man and a woman truly love each other . . .' by Jean Vanier from *Man and Woman, He Made Them* (DLT 1985).

Let's Play Mums and Dads

'It is difficult for the husband . . .' from *Childbirth: a Christian Perspective* by Jenny Cooke (Grove Booklet, Ethics No. 43, 1981).

'The Roots of Male Sensuality' by Archibald D. Hart from *The Sexual Man* (Word Publishing 1994).

'I Don't Like Men' by Stewart Henderson from *Homeland* (Hodder and Stoughton 1993).

'They Were Our Children Too, Grief of Fathers Bereaved by a Cot Death' (The Foundation for the Study of Infant Deaths 1994).

'Hero' by Marion Pitman from *Lunch with Veronica* (Eating People Publications 1988).

Like Brother and Sister

'Boys make fun of girls . . .' by Paul Tournier from *The Gift of Feeling* (SCM 1981).

'You're only a Girl' by W. P. Livingstone from *The White Queen of Okoyong* (Hodder and Stoughton , n. d.).

We're Just Good Friends

'Platonic love' by Archibald D. Hart from *The Sexual Man* (Word Publishing 1994).

'A man needs to feel . . .' by Paul Tournier from *Marriage Difficulties* (SCM 1967).

'For all kinds of reasons . . .' by Ronald Rolheiser from *Forgotten among the Lilies*, (Spire 1990).

Love Makes the World Go Round

'On Falling in Love' by Stewart Henderson from *Assembled in Britain* (Harper Collins Publishers Ltd 1986).

'I Knew You Once Without Enchantment' © 1984 by Noel Coward, reprinted by permission of Michael Imison Playwrights Ltd.

'Bloody Men' by Wendy Cope from *Serious Concerns* (Faber and Faber, 1992).

Horse and Carriage

'I Am Lonely' from *The Rector's Wife* by Joanna Trollope (Bloomsbury/Black Swan 1991), reprinted by permission of the Peters Fraser and Dunlop Group Ltd.

'Confronting the Niggles' by Mary Reid from *Married to the Church*, edited by Shelagh Brown (Triangle 1983).

'The Holiday' by Ella Wheeler Wilcox (1850–1919), from *The Oxford Book of Marriage*, edited by Helge Rubinstein (OUP 1990).

'Episode of Decay' by Witter Bynner, from *The Oxford Book of Marriage*, edited by Helge Rubenstein (OUP 1990).

'Noting that he had two birds . . . ' from *Healing the Masculine Soul* by Gordon Dalbey, (Word 1988).

'The Injustice of It All' from *My Son's A Doctor (The Doctor's Post,* 14th July, 1995).

'Marriage' by Elaine Feinstein from *Some Unease and Angels: Selected Poems* (Hutchinson 1977) reprinted with the permission of the Carcanet Press Ltd.

'I'm in the Dark with You' by Stewart Henderson from *Homeland* (Hodder and Stoughton 1993).

Fancies, Follies and Fantasies

'And do you not know that you are Eve?' from *De Cultu Feminarum, On Female Dress* by Tertullian (160–225 AD).

'Temptation' by G. A. Studdert Kennedy from *The Unutterable Beauty* (Hodder and Stoughton 1941).

'By far the most common reason' by Archibald D. Hart from *The Sexual Man* (Word 1994).

'Merriment is an antidote' by Adrian Thatcher from *Liberating Sex* (SPCK 1993).

'Elegy to Love' by John Donne, Elegy XIX, published 1633.

'No Sex Please, We're Christians' by Michele Guinness, first published in *Woman Alive* magazine, January 1995.

Some Are Just More Equal then Others

'Man is active' by Aristotle (384–322 BC) from *Politics*, Bk 1.

'What men expect mostly from women' by Paul Tournier from *The Gift of Feeling* (SCM 1981).

Excerpt by Susan Howatch from *Absolute Truths* (Harper Collins 1994).

'Women with pastoral . . .' by Elaine Storkey from *What's Right with Feminism* (SPCK 1985).

'The Missionary Wife' by Joy Turner Tuggy from *The Missionary Wife and her Work* (Moody Press 1966).

'The missionary women's story' by Lavinia Byrne from *The Hidden Journey* (SPCK 1993).

'The shortage of men. . . .' by David Pawson from *Leadership is Male* (Highland 1988).

'Dogs have four legs' by Michael Harper from *Equal And Different* (Hodder and Stoughton 1994).

'We are blind to the familiar' by Roy McCloughry from *Men and Masculinity* (Hodder and Stoughton 1992).

'My daughter-in-law is an artist . . .' by Paul Tournier from *The Gift of Feeling* (SCM 1981).

'Some of the women in our group . . .' from *A Fearful Symmetry: The Complementariness of Men and Woman in Ministry*, with a Foreword by John V. Taylor (SPCK 1992).

'A Liturgy of Reconciliation' by Chung Hyun Kyung from *Struggle to be the Sun Again: Introducing Asian Women's Theology* (SCM 1990), reprinted from *In God's Image*, December 1984, an Asian women's theological journal.

The Battle of the Sexes

Quotes by Deborah Tannen from *You Just Don't Understand Me* (Virago 1992).

'Men are more proud . . .' by Paul Tournier from *Marriage Difficulties* (SCM 1967).

'The fear of one another . . .' by Gordon Dalbey from *Healing the Masculine Soul* (Word Publishing 1988).

'He Is a Mysterious Island' by Paul Tournier from *Marriage Difficulties* (SCM 1967).

'Visiting the Specialist' by Evangeline Paterson from *Lucifer at the Fair* (Taxus 1991).

Oh What Needless Pain We Bear

'The Real Problem' by Adrian Plass from *Clearing Away the Rubbish* (Kingsway Publications 1988).

'Three Rounds with an Amateur Tyrant' by Stewart Henderson from *A Giant's Scrapbook* (Hodder and Stoughton 1989).

'Battered into Submission: The tragedy of Wife Abuse in the Christian Home', by James and Phyllis Alsdurf (Highland 1990).

'As soon as a husband . . .' by Paul Tournier from *Marriage Difficulties* (SCM 1967).

'Where Are the Men?' Excerpt from 'At the End of the Second Millennium – Where Are the Women?' the Henry Martyn Lecture, given at the Evangelical Missionary Alliance Conference, 1994 by Elaine Storkey, and published in *Contributions to Christian Feminism* (Christian Impact, 1995).

Vive la Différence

'The Churching of Women' by Bishop Hugh Montefiore from the *Church Times*, April 28 1995.

'Even Our Consciences Are Different!' by Paul Tournier from *Marriage Difficulties* (SCM 1967).

'Civilisation' by Evangeline Paterson from *Bringing the Water Hyacinth to Africa* (Taxus 1983).

'Lenten Thoughts' by John Betjeman from *A Nip in the Air* in *Enlarged Collected Works* (John Murray 1979).

'A milieu with both men and women . . .' from *Man and Woman, He Made Them* by Jean Vanier (DLT 1985).

'The Psychiatrist's Song' by A. S. J. Tessimond from *Voices in a Giant City* (Heinemann 1947), courtesy of Hubert Nicholson.

Without You

'I love thee with a love I seemed to lose' by Elizabeth Barrett Browning (1806–61) from *Sonnets from the Portuguese*.

'Saffiyah' by Najwa Farah from *The Colour of Courage* (Christians Aware 1991).

'Joys that Sting' by C. S. Lewis from *Shadowlands* by Brian Sibley (Hodder and Stoughton 1985).

Every effort has been made to trace and contact copyright holders. Any omissions are inadvertent and we apologize to those concerned.